Corporate Acquisitions and Mergers in Russia

Corporate Acquisitions and Mergers in Russia

Second Edition

Andrei Dontsov
Irina Dmitrieva
Natalia Nikitina

White & Case

This book was originally published as a chapter in Corporate Acquisitions and Mergers.

General Editor: Peter Begg

Wolters Kluwer

Published by:
Kluwer Law International B.V.
PO Box 316
2400 AH Alphen aan den Rijn
The Netherlands
E-mail: international-sales@wolterskluwer.com
Website: lrus.wolterskluwer.com

Sold and distributed in North, Central and South America by:
Wolters Kluwer Legal & Regulatory U.S.
7201 McKinney Circle
Frederick, MD 21704
United States of America
Email: customer.service@wolterskluwer.com

Sold and distributed in all other countries by:
Air Business Subscriptions
Rockwood House
Haywards Heath
West Sussex
RH16 3DH
United Kingdom
Email: international-customerservice@wolterskluwer.com

ISBN 978-94-035-2763-5

e-Book: ISBN 978-94-035-2764-2
web-PDF: ISBN 978-94-035-2765-9

This title is available on www.kluwerlawonline.com

Contents

White & Case

White & Case is a leading global law firm with 2 200 lawyers based in forty-four offices across thirty countries. Since the opening of our office in Moscow in 1991, White & Case has established itself as one of the leading law firms on the ground in Russia and the CIS. The office focuses on Corporate/M&A, Banking & Finance, Capital Markets, Energy & Utilities, Real Estate, Dispute Resolution, Antitrust and Tax matters. The office consistently wins praise from clients and independent observers of the legal market in Russia, including *Chambers, The Legal 500* and *IFLR1000,* who unanimously rank us in the top tiers across all our key practice areas.

White & Case LLC www.whitecase.com

4 Romanov Pereulok 125009 Moscow, Russia

Tel.: +7 495 787 3000

Fax: +7 495 787 3001

Partners: Andrei Dontsov, Irina Dmitrieva and Natalia Nikitina

1 ECONOMIC, POLITICAL AND CULTURAL ASPECTS

1.1 General Comments on Country Profile

[01] The Russian Federation, or Russia *(Rossiya* in Russian), is a sovereign federal republic bordering eighteen countries and spanning eleven time zones. It is the largest country in the world in terms of territory.

[02] The population of Russia is approximately 146.78 m (2.05% of the world's population) and ranks 9th in the world by population size. Russia's capital and largest city is Moscow (12.6 m inhabitants) and is within the top-10 largest cities in the world.

1.2 Government and Political System

[03] Russia has a federal system of government and is divided into federation 'subjects', comprising republics, *krais* (territories), *oblasts* (regions), autonomous *oblast* (autonomous region), autonomous *okrugs* (districts) and cities of federal importance. Each of the constituent entities (federation subjects) is in turn divided into municipalities, cities and towns.

[04] The Constitution of the Russian Federation provides for a tripartite governmental structure in which the power of the state is divided between the executive, legislative and judicial branches, each branch being independent of the others. The Constitution also establishes a federal system, allocating responsibilities between federal, sub-federal and local authorities.

[05] The executive branch consists of the President and the Government of the Russian Federation. The Government consists of the Prime Minister, deputy prime ministers, and ministers of federal ministries, appointed by the President.

[06] The legislative branch is the Federal Assembly (or the Parliament), which consists of the State Duma (the lower chamber) and the Federation Council (the upper chamber).

[07] The judicial branch is made up of several main types of state courts. The Constitutional Court has jurisdiction over matters relating to the interpretation of the Constitution, including the constitutionality of federal laws, decrees of the President, and resolutions of the Government. Judicial authority in commercial, civil, administrative, criminal and other matters is vested in the Supreme Court of the Russian Federation and lower courts, made up of commercial courts and courts of general jurisdiction.

[08] Russia's Constitutional Court has jurisdiction over matters relating to the interpretation of the Constitution, including the constitutionality of federal laws, presidential decrees, and resolutions of the Government. Judicial authority is otherwise vested in the Supreme Court and lower courts of general jurisdiction in civil, criminal, administrative and other matters.

[09] Russia is a successor to the Soviet Union and maintains diplomatic relations with over 175 countries. It is currently a member of many international organizations, including the United Nations (UN), where it is a permanent member of the Security Council.

[10] Since 1992, Russia has been a member of the International Monetary Fund (IMF) and the International Bank for Reconstruction and Development (also known as the 'World Bank'). Russia is a member of the International Finance Corporation (IFC) and participates as a donor in the International Development Association. Russia is also a member of the European Bank for Reconstruction and Development (EBRD), the Soviet Union being one of its founders. EBRD has provided several billion euros of funding to projects in Russia.

[11] Since 1992, Russia has had working contacts with the Organisation for Economic Co-operation and Development (OECD). Russia has been granted observer status on the working bodies of the OECD. On 30 November 2007, the OECD Council approved the 'roadmap to accession' for the Russian Federation. The accession is still in process.

[12] In 2012, Russia became a full member of the World Trade Organization (WTO). Now all WTO agreements and commitments apply to Russia, with a small number of transitional periods in areas of particular sensitivity (e.g., financial services and insurance).

1.3 Legal System

[13] Russia is a civil law jurisdiction and court practice formally does not constitute a source of law here. However, the Constitutional Court precedents interpreting the Constitution are binding for Russian courts. Importantly, commercial courts are obliged to follow the Supreme Court's and the former Supreme Commercial Court's legal positions as stipulated by law.

[14] In particular, the resolutions of the Plenum of the Supreme Court and the effective resolutions of the former Plenum of the Supreme Commercial Court are binding. The resolutions of the Presidium of the Supreme Court that change current court practice could be used as grounds for the reconsideration of a court decision that has become legally binding. The effective resolutions of the former Presidium of the Supreme Commercial Court also serve as a precedent.[1] The

[1] Determination or change of interpretation of a legal norm by a resolution of the Plenum or by the Presidium of the Supreme Court, if the relevant decision of the Supreme Court specifies the possibility of review of effective court decisions by virtue of this occurrence, serve as a ground for the review of lower court decisions due to new circumstances (Art. 311(3)(5) of the Commercial Procedure Code). The rationale of court decisions may contain references to resolutions of the Plenum

Supreme Court summarizes court practice and issues court practice explanations in the form of overviews (the former Supreme Commercial Court also issued information letters). Such explanations are used as interpretative recommendations and guidelines for lower courts when dealing with similar issues. It should be noted that, in practice, not only the Supreme Courts' decisions but also the lower courts' practice is considered by courts when rendering decisions.

[15] Enforcement of contractual and other rights through the courts is relatively efficient in Russia.[2] This is due to many factors. Although the duration of the proceedings depends on the effectiveness of the judge and his/her workload, certain time standards set by the law make case management in Russia, one of the fastest. In general, it takes around three months for a Commercial Court of First Instance to consider a simple case if no expert opinion is necessary, around four months if an expert opinion is required and the parties do not request expert witness testimony in court, and around five months if they request expert witnesses to attend the trial.

[16] The availability of electronic filing and electronic case management contributes to the efficiency of commercial courts. Some options for electronic case management are also available in courts of general jurisdiction. All commercial court judgments (and procedural rulings) are published in a database on the website of the Supreme Commercial Court (http://kad.arbitr.ru/). Court judgments in civil cases are sometimes published without the parties' names (www.sudrf.ru). The efficiency of judicial processes is also due to the availability of such mechanisms as pre-trial attachments of assets. However, in general, chances to attach the defendant's assets are higher after filing a statement of claim.

[17] Russia has a civil law system. The Russian Civil Code is based on European codes. The bankruptcy law is based on German statutory law, while the securities law was significantly influenced by the United States (US) model. Generally recognized principles or customs of international law and international treaties are also an integral part of the legal system and generally override domestic regulation. Given Russia's status as a federal state, private law is a matter of federal jurisdiction. While statutory law is more important than judicial precedents, the gradual convergence with a common law type of legal system is giving the precedents increasingly more weight.

(Presidium) of the Supreme Court and the effective resolutions of the Plenum (Presidium) of the former Supreme Commercial Court on issues of judicial interpretation (Art. 170(4)(3) of the Commercial Procedure Code).

[2] According to the World Bank's survey 'Doing Business 2020' on enforcement of commercial contracts, Russia's *Quality of Judicial Processes Index* is relatively high – 72.2 out of a possible score of 100. It is ranked 21st out of 189 economies on the ease of enforcing contracts (*See*: http://www.doingbusiness.org/data/exploreeconomies/russia#enforcing-contracts).

2 THE REGULATORY FRAMEWORK FOR M&A

2.1 Business Vehicles: General Overview

[18] Russian law differentiates between commercial and non-commercial legal entities. Commercial legal entities are created to generate profits, whereas non-commercial legal entities do not pursue this aim and do not distribute profits among their participants. Both groups have a number of forms with certain particularities. Whereas some forms are commonly used in business, others may appear in legislation only. Both commercial and non-commercial legal entities are subject to state registration. Registration is carried out by the Federal Tax Service of the Russian Federation (the '*Tax Authorities*'). The registration procedure is governed by Federal Law No. 129-FZ 'On State Registration of Legal Entities and Individual Entrepreneurs', dated 8 August 2001.

[19] Information on all legal entities registered in Russia is entered by the Tax Authorities into the Unified State Register of Legal Entities (USRLE) (the '*Companies' Register*'). The Companies' Register is the official public database containing information on all legal entities registered in the Russian Federation. The legal entities operating in Russia are required to file certain documents with the Companies' Register (e.g., information about participants in limited liability companies, information about the general director) and make sure that the information reflected in the Companies' Register is up to date.

2.2 Commercial Legal Entities

[20] Russian law provides for various forms of commercial legal entities. Commercial companies in Russia may be set up in any of the following legal forms enumerated in the Civil Code of the Russian Federation (the '*Civil Code*'):

(i) Business companies:
  - joint stock companies (public joint stock companies and non-public joint stock companies), and
  - limited liability companies;

(ii) Business partnerships (full partnerships and trust partnerships),

(iii) Farming enterprises,

(iv) Production cooperatives,

(v) State or municipally owned unitary enterprises.

[21] Limited liability companies and joint stock companies are the two most popular forms used in business.

2.3 Non-commercial Legal Entities

[22] Legal entities created for purposes other than to generate profit are non-commercial legal entities. Russian law distinguishes the following forms of non-commercial legal entities: consumer cooperatives (cooperatives of households, garages, garden owners, societies for mutual insurance, credit cooperatives, rental funds, and agricultural consumer cooperatives); non-governmental organizations (political parties, professional unions, and territorial citizens unions); social movements; associations (unions) (non-commercial partnerships, self-regulated organizations, employers' associations, labour unions, chambers for trade and commerce, notary chambers, etc.); partnerships of real estate owners, Cossack societies, small indigenous groups, charity funds, state and municipal institutions, autonomous non-commercial organizations, religious organizations, advocate chambers and bar associations, etc.

2.4 Overview of Joint Stock Companies and Limited Liability Companies

[23] The vast majority of commercial legal entities established in Russia are limited liability companies. Limited liability companies are commonly referred to by the Russian abbreviation 'OOO' or its English abbreviation 'LLC', and joint stock companies by the Russian abbreviation 'AO' or its English abbreviation 'JSC'. Both have much in common with respect to general registration procedures and corporate management and enjoy the same legal capacity to conduct business. Below we review the distinctions between these two forms.

[24] There are two types of JSCs: public JSCs (referred to as '*PAO*' or '*PJSC*') and non-public JSCs (referred to as simply '*AO*' or '*JSC*'). The particular type of a JSC must be specified in its charter and also indicated in its name. It is relatively easy for a non-public company to become public – such resolution requires 75% vote of all shareholders (and not only those present in the general meeting); however, transformation of the public company into a non-public requires approval of 95% of all shareholders of the joint stock company.

[25] Only a public JSC can issue shares to the public (through a public offering) and have its shares traded publicly on terms and conditions specified by the securities market laws.

2.5 Incorporation

[26] Both JSCs and LLCs are registered by the Tax Authorities as the main regulatory body responsible for legal entities' registration in Russia. However, depending on the sector in which a particular legal entity is going to operate, other authorities may also need to be involved. For example, the main registration

authority for banks and insurance companies is the Central Bank, and the information about such registration is still entered into the Companies' Register.

[27] JSCs and LLCs operate on the basis of their charters (in Russian – *ustav*), which are equivalent to articles of association in other jurisdictions. The charter sets out the principal terms of the JSC's or LLC's internal organization, including the competence of the company's management bodies, the rights and obligations of the shareholders/participants, limitations (if any) on the authority of the company's chief executive officer (CEO), the authorized share/charter capital, the procedure for increasing the charter capital and other provisions relating to the internal organization of the relevant legal entity. The charter has to be filed and registered with the relevant local branch of the Tax Authorities.

[28] The statutory period for registration of a legal entity is five days after all of the documents required for the incorporation have been submitted. It may take a significant amount of time to collect all the necessary documents, especially if the founder is a foreign entity. However, it usually takes three to four weeks after registration for a company to become fully operational (as additional time is required to complete post-registration procedures such as obtaining documents from non-budgetary funds, manufacturing the company's seal, opening bank accounts and providing various notices to state authorities).

[29] Any person (upon payment of a nominal fee) can obtain an extract containing basic corporate information in relation to any Russian entity from the Companies' Register. Copies of the documents kept on file regarding entities in the Companies' Register (such as a company's charter) can also be obtained by any person. For example, a copy of the charter of a company or hard copy excerpt from the Companies' Register in respect of a particular legal entity can be obtained from the Tax Authorities for a fee of RUB200 (approx. USD3). Electronic versions of excerpts from the Companies' Register in respect of particular legal entities are provided by the Tax Authorities free of charge through the official website of the Tax Authorities (https://egrul.nalog.ru/).

2.6 Charter Capital

2.6.1 Charter Capital Requirements

[30] The charter capital is the minimum value of the company's property securing the rights of its creditors. Russian law requires that LLCs and JSCs maintain the statutory minimum value of charter capital, which for LLCs and non-public JSCs is RUB10 000 (approx. USD179) and for public JSCs RUB100 000 (approx. USD1 670). At the same time, regulations in specific sectors (such as financial services) may require a higher value of the minimum charter capital.

[31] Upon the company's establishment, the charter capital must be paid within the statutory terms: in LLCs – in full within four months (or a shorter period if so provided in the charter); in a JSC – at least 50% within the first three months and the remaining part within twelve months.

[32] The minimum charter capital must be paid in cash; the amount of the charter capital exceeding the minimum may be paid in cash or in kind.

[33] The value of contributions to the charter capital paid for the participatory interest/shares may not be less than the nominal value of the respective participatory interest/shares; however, it may exceed that value, resulting in a share premium (such share premium is recorded for accounting purposes as 'additional capital').

[34] The value of in-kind contributions must be determined by an independent appraiser and then by the participants/shareholders (or supervisory board if applicable). However, the latter valuation may not exceed the appraiser's valuation.

2.6.2 Net Asset Value

[35] If as of the end of the second or each subsequent financial year the value of the net assets of the company falls below its charter capital, the company must, within the term and pursuant to the procedure established by the LLC Law and JSC Law, respectively, increase the value of its net assets to the amount not lower than the amount of the charter capital or register a reduction of its charter capital.[3]

[36] If the net assets value becomes less than the minimum amount of the charter capital, the company is subject to liquidation.

[37] The net asset value is calculated based on the company's accounting records as the difference between the company's assets (other than outstanding receivables from participants/shareholders to the charter capital) and liabilities (other than future income).[4]

2.6.3 Contributions to the Company's Property (Without Charter Capital Increase)

[38] The charter may require participants/shareholders to contribute to the company's property upon the General Partners Meeting/General Shareholders Meeting decision. Such contributions do not change the charter capital and do not alter the size of participatory interests/shareholding. This is a convenient way to provide funding to the company in an accelerated manner. The contributions may be in cash or in kind.

[39] Notably, for Russian tax purposes, contributions to the company's property are not recognized as a part of the acquisition cost of the participatory interest/shares. Such contributions are often used for increasing the net asset value up to the charter capital amount.

---

[3] Articles 90, 99 of the Civil Code.

[4] Order of the Ministry of Finance No. 84n dated 28 August 2014.

2.6.4 Reserve Fund

[40] A JSC must have a reserve fund in the amount of at least 5% of the charter capital by forming it with contributions of at least 5% of annual net profits.[5]

[41] For LLCs, reserve funds are optional.

2.7 Rights to Participatory Interests in LLC and Rights to Shares in JSC

2.7.1 LLC

[42] Participatory interests are not deemed to be securities and do not require registration with the securities market regulatory authority (the Central Bank). The information about participatory interests is recorded in the USRLE that is maintained by the tax authorities. The LLC also must maintain a list of participants maintained, which also contains details of the par value of each participatory interest belonging to each participant.

[43] LLCs cannot have more than fifty participants. If the number of participants in an LLC exceeds fifty, the LLC must be transformed into a JSC.

[44] The LLC Law requires any transaction involving the transfer of participatory interests in an LLC to be notarized (i.e., certified by a public notary in Russian). Failure to do so will result in the relevant transaction being invalid. Rights to participatory interests are deemed transferred to the new owner upon registration in the Companies' Register.

2.7.2 JSC

[45] The creation of a JSC involves the issuance of shares, which are deemed to be securities. Issued shares must be registered with the Central Bank. Shares only exist in non-documentary form and title to the shares is recorded in the shareholder register maintained by an independent licensed share registrar (as opposed to LLCs, where the legal entity itself maintains a list of participants). The shares in a JSC may be ordinary or preferred. The law allows only one class of ordinary shares, but provides that there may be several classes of preferred shares.

[46] The shares in a public JSC may be offered to an unlimited number of potential buyers and may be traded publicly on stock exchanges. The largest stock exchange in Russia is the Moscow Exchange (MOEX), which was created following the merger of the Russian Trading System (RTS) and the Moscow Interbank Currency Exchange (MICEX) in 2011.

[5] Article 35(1) of the JSC Law.

[47] No restrictions (such as right of first refusal) may apply to the transfer of shares in public JSCs.

[48] There are specific corporate procedures (mandatory tender offer (MTO) and squeeze-out) that are applicable to public JSCs. Note that these provisions of Russian law are mandatory and may not be derogated from by agreement of the parties involved. Both procedures are discussed in detail in section 'Specific Rules on Public Takeovers' below.

[49] *Non-Public JSCs.* The shares of a non-public JSC may not be publicly traded.

[50] All transactions with shares in non-public JSCs are considered to be private deals, and a transfer of the ownership title to the shares in a non-public JSC is recorded by an independent registrar maintaining the shareholder register of the company.

[51] Also, when new shares are issued, the shareholders of a non-public JSC enjoy a pre-emption right in relation to the newly issued shares pro rata their shareholdings, in cases where a shareholder voted against the share issuance or was not present at the meeting approving the share issuance.

2.8 Shareholders Liability

[52] The scope of liability of LLC participants and JSC shareholders is similar.

[53] LLC participants and JSC shareholders are generally not liable for the debts of the company, and their risk of loss as participants or shareholders is limited to the value of the participatory interests/shares that they own.

[54] Participants and shareholders who have not fully paid for their participatory interests in an LLC or shares in a JSC are jointly and severally liable for the liabilities of the company to the extent of the unpaid portion of their participatory interests or shares.

[55] In addition, participants and shareholders may be liable for the debts of the LLC or the JSC if their actions or failure to act results in the insolvency or bankruptcy of the company.

[56] The Civil Code sets forth the main principles of the autonomy and limited liability of each legal entity: a legal entity owns property and is liable for its debts only to the extent of the property it owns (Article 48); a founder (participant) of a legal entity is not liable for the legal entity's obligations, and the legal entity is not liable for the participant's obligations, unless otherwise provided by law or the foundation documents (Article 56);[6] and a subsidiary is not liable for the debts of the parent company (Article 67.3(2)).

[6] For example, the partners of a general partnership jointly and severally guarantee the debts of the partnership.

[57] At the same time, the persons that *de facto* control a legal entity may be held liable for damages suffered by the legal entity if such damages were caused by fault of the controlling person.

[58] *Bankruptcy.* If a debtor is deemed insolvent (bankrupt) as a result of actions and/or omissions of persons controlling the debtor (shareholders or other persons entitled to give binding instructions to the debtor or otherwise direct the activities of the debtor), such controlling persons will be jointly liable for the liabilities of the debtor if the debtor's property is insufficient to cover the debts.[7] Similarly, parent companies are jointly liable for the debts of their subsidiaries if the subsidiary becomes insolvent due to the fault of the parent company.[8]

[59] However, the joint liability applies only if the insolvency (bankruptcy) of a company was caused by actions or omissions of the controlling persons who knew in advance that their actions would result in the company's insolvency (bankruptcy).[9] To establish the liability of the controlling persons, it is necessary to prove that: (1) they exercised control over the debtor; (2) they performed or authorized certain actions to withhold assets from the debtor and were aware that such actions would lead to its insolvency; and (3) the actions actually caused the insolvency.

[60] *Transactions.* A parent company and a subsidiary company are jointly liable for the transactions executed by the subsidiary if such transactions have been executed to fulfil the instructions of the parent company or with the consent of the parent company (except for transactions approved by the parent company at the general participants meeting of the subsidiary). The participants (shareholders) of a subsidiary company are entitled to claim damages caused by the parent company to the subsidiary company.[10]

[61] The law requires all legal entities are required to collect (or take actions to collect), keep and annually update information[11] on their beneficial owners, and disclose such information upon request to the federal government agencies and bodies, including the Tax Authorities. For this purpose, a beneficial owner is defined as an individual holding, directly or indirectly, more than 25% in the charter capital in a legal entity, or controlling the activities of the entity. Legal entities that fail to provide information to the state authorities on their beneficial owners upon request may be punished by a fine of up to RUB500 000 (approx. USD8 000).

[7] Section III.2 of the Law on Bankruptcy.

[8] Article 67.3(2) of the Civil Code, Art. 6 of the LLC Law, Art. 6 of the JSC Law.

[9] Article 3 of the JSC Law, Art. 3 of the LLC Law.

[10] Article 67.3(2, 3) of the Civil Code, Art. 6 of the JSC Law, Art. 6 of the LLC Law.

[11] Name of the beneficial owner, citizenship, date of birth, ID information, residential address and taxpayer ID. In accordance with the Law on Fighting Legalization of Illegal income and Terrorism Finance No. 115-FZ of 7 August 2001.

2.9 General Capacity of Legal Entities and Ultra Vires Doctrine

[62] LLCs and JSCs do not have any distinctions in respect of legal capacity. By general rule, the legal capacity of a legal entity arises at the moment of its inclusion in the Companies' Register and ceases at the moment an entry is made on its termination.

[63] All legal entities have the right to perform activities allowed by law and listed in their charters. Certain activities under Russian law may require a special license or permission, or membership in self-regulating organizations.

[64] Russian law also allows a company's charter to restrict the company's capacity or the capacity of its general director to perform certain activities or transactions. Transactions executed in violation of such limitations are voidable and may be held invalid if the other party to the transaction knew or should have known about the prohibition.[12]

2.10 Management Structure

[65] A JSC or LLC can have a two- or three-tier management structure. In a three-tier structure, the management bodies comprise: (i) the general shareholders or participants meeting (ii) the board of directors and (iii) the executive body's CEO and the management board. The board of directors is mandatory for all public JSCs and non-public JSCs with more than fifty shareholders and is optional for LLCs and non-public JSCs with fewer than fifty shareholders.

[66] The participants or shareholders meeting is the supreme governing body of a company and makes the major decisions.

[67] There are two types of GSM/GPM: annual general meetings and extraordinary general meetings. An LLC/JSC must hold an annual general meeting each year within the time period provided in its charter, but not earlier than two months and no later than six months after the end of the company's reporting year (i.e., by 1 July). All meetings other than the annual general meeting are considered to be extraordinary.

[68] Both the JSC Law and the LLC Law[13] set forth a list of issues that may be decided by a general participants' meeting or general shareholders' meeting and allows companies to extend that body's competence in the company's charter. In public JSCs, the competence of the shareholders' meeting is defined by law and cannot be changed by the charter of the company.

[69] There is no quorum requirement for a general participants' meeting. Most decisions of a general participants' meeting of an LLC require simple majority

[12] Article 173 of the Civil Code.

[13] *See* the chapter on laws affecting M&A.

approval of the company's participants (as opposed to those attending the meeting), unless the company's charter establishes a higher voting requirement. Decisions on material issues require two-thirds vote of all participants of the company (e.g., amendment of an LLC's charter), or a unanimous vote (e.g., reorganization of the company; liquidation of the company; amendment of the company's charter to provide termination of or limiting the rights of the participants in the company compared to those provided in the LLC Law; amendment of the company's charter to change the procedure for the distribution of profits).

[70] In a JSC, a shareholders' meeting 'has a quorum' if shareholders holding in aggregate more than 50% of the voting shares of the company participated in the meeting. In general, decisions of a general shareholders' meeting are adopted by a simple majority vote of the holders of voting shares participating in the meeting. However, certain decisions require adoption by a 75% vote of the holders of voting shares participating in the meeting (e.g., amendment of the company's charter; reorganization of the company; liquidation of the company; determination of the quantity, nominal value and type of shares issued by the company and the rights conferred by the shares; redemption of the company's shares; approval of certain major transactions).

[71] A participant/shareholder may participate in general participants' meetings directly or through a representative acting under a power of attorney.

[72] *A board of directors (supervisory board)* is optional for an LLC or JSC with fewer than fifty shareholders.

[73] A company's board of directors (or supervisory board) is responsible for the management of its activities, except for those issues reserved for the authority of the general participants' meeting.

[74] The size of the board of directors of an LLC and JSC and its scope of authority are determined by the company's charter. In a JSC, the board of directors must have at least five members. The minimum number of members for a JSC with more than 1 000 holders of voting shares is seven, and the minimum number of members for a JSC with more than 10 000 holders of voting shares is nine.

[75] In LLCs, the procedure and voting thresholds for electing the supervisory board's members are set by the charter.[14] In a non-public JSC, members of the supervisory board are elected by cumulative voting unless the charter provides otherwise.[15] In a public JSC, members of the supervisory board are elected only by

[14] Article 66.3(3)(para. 5) of the Civil Code, Art. 37(9) of the LLC Law.

[15] Article 66(4) of the JSC Law currently provides for mandatory cumulative vote of a GSM for the election of the board. However, pursuant to Art. 66.3(2)(para. 5) of the Civil Code, the charter of a non-public company can establish a procedure for adopting decisions at a GM which is different from the statutory procedure (provided that such procedure does not deprive the participants/shareholders of the right to take part in the GM and to receive information about it). This provision of the Civil Code may be used to justify an alternative voting method for the election of the board being set out in a non-pubic company's charter.

cumulative voting.[16] In cumulative voting, the number of shares held by each shareholder is multiplied by the number of persons to be elected to the board and each shareholder may cast all the votes thus obtained for one candidate or allocate them among two or more candidates. When re-electing a board elected by cumulative vote, the entire board must be re-elected, i.e., individual members of the board cannot be replaced by the shareholders.

[76] *The executive authority* performs the day-to-day management of a company's affairs and may be either a sole executive body (either an individual, usually holding the title of general director, or a management company) or a sole executive body acting together with a collegial executive body (usually referred to as the management board). If a company's charter provides for both such bodies, the general director serves as the chairman of the management board. The size, functions and procedures of the management board are determined by the charter and internal documents of the company.

[77] The general director (or an external management company), as well as members of the management board, is appointed and dismissed by the general participants' meeting unless the company's charter delegates this authority to the board of directors.

[78] Normally, the authority of the executive body extends to all matters not within the scope of the authority of the board of directors or the general participants' meeting.

[79] Recent amendments of Russian law allow several persons to act on behalf of a company (e.g., several general directors acting under the company's charter). In such cases, the company's charter must specify the powers of each of those persons, and the relevant information about each of the persons acting on behalf of the company must be included in the Companies' Register. Despite these amendments, most companies still prefer to have one general director.

2.11 Duties and Liability of Management Bodies

[80] Rules governing duties and liability of management bodies of LLCs and JSCs are similar.

[81] Russian law requires members of the board of directors, the general director, members of the management board and an external management company, or an external manager of a company to act in the interests of the company reasonably and in good faith.

[82] As a general rule, any person who acts on behalf of a company (both LLC and JSC) under the law or the charter may be held liable. Such persons include: (i) the

[16] Article 66(4) of the JSC Law. In cumulative voting, the number of shares held by each shareholder is multiplied by the number of persons to be elected to the board, and each shareholder may cast all votes thus obtained for one candidate or divide them among two or more candidates.

general director; (ii) members of the board of directors; (iii) members of the management board; (iv) the chief accountant (who bears liability for the formation of the accounting policy, the performance of the accounting, and the timely provision of accounting reports); and (v) other officers (i.e., employees performing organizational and management functions as well as administrative functions). It is important to note that the termination of powers does not affect the possibility of holding the managers or directors liable (provided the offence is committed when the managers or directors held the relevant positions and the statute of limitations has not expired). Any agreement on the exclusion or limitation of liability of a person entitled to act on behalf of the company as well as the members of the company's collegial executive body for bad faith actions, and in a public company for bad faith and unreasonable actions, is void.

[83] The Civil Code (Article 53.1) establishes the liability of a person who de facto can determine the company's activities, including giving mandatory instructions to the persons acting on behalf of the company and the members of its executive bodies. Any agreement on the exclusion or limitation of liability of such person is void.

[84] Directors and managers are liable for losses sustained by a legal entity through their fault (whether by action or failure to act). Additionally, there may be cases when the directors and managers will be liable for losses sustained by the shareholders as well. If the decision that caused the losses was adopted by a collegial body, the liability of the members of the collegial body is joint and several. However, if a member of a collegial body voted against the action that caused the losses or, acting in good faith, did not participate in the voting, the member will not be liable for the losses caused by the decision.

[85] As a general rule, directors and managers may not be held liable with respect to: (i) decisions on issues of an advisory, organizational or technical nature (e.g., on taking inventory, on the composition of the management bodies, on business plans, or on foundation documents), or (ii) decisions on increasing the charter capital of a legal entity. While this is not directly established by law, in such cases it is difficult to prove that the relevant decisions really caused losses to a legal entity.

2.12 Dividends and Profits Distribution

[86] LLC participants receive income in the form of net profits distributed by the LLC, and the shareholders of a JSC in the form of dividends distributed by the JSC. Both are paid out of the company's net profit, which is defined as the company's profits calculated based on the Russian financial accounting rules and after the payment of taxes. The distribution can take place quarterly, semi-annually or annually.

[87] Decisions on distribution of net profits of an LLC and dividends of a JSC are made by the general meeting of participants/shareholders.

[88] Net profits in LLCs are distributed among the participants on a pro rata basis depending on the value of their participatory interest unless otherwise determined in an LLC's charter or the relevant decision of participants on net profits distribution. In JSCs, dividends are declared as a fixed amount payable per one share.

[89] Companies cannot decide to distribute profit in the following circumstances: (i) before the charter capital has been paid in full; (ii) before the company pays for participation interests or shares in the case of buyback when required by the LLC Law or the JSC Law; (iii) if the company meets the insolvency test or will become insolvent as a result of payment of dividends; (iv) at the moment the relevant decision is adopted, the value of the company's net assets is less than its charter capital and reserve fund, or would be less than such amount as a result of such decision, and (v) in the case of a JSC, until the dividends on preferred shares have been paid (if the amount of such dividends is set out in the charter).

2.13 Reporting, Information Disclosure

[90] The legal basis for the financial accounting rules is Federal Law No. 402-FZ 'On Accounting', dated 6 December 2011. It sets forth the basic principles of Russian accounting.

[91] The basic financial accounting year in Russia is the calendar year. The first accounting year for a legal entity starts from the date of its state registration and ends on 31 December of the same calendar year. However, if a legal entity was registered after 1 October, its first accounting year ends on 31 December of the following calendar year.

[92] Every Russian legal entity is required to make quarterly and annual filings of financial statements drawn from the accounting records. These financial statements (the base currency of which is the Russian ruble) consist of a balance sheet, profit and loss statement, report on changes in capital, cash flow statement, attachments thereto, and explanatory notes. Companies furnish the financial statements to their shareholders and participants and also file the statements with the Tax Authorities.

[93] An LLC/JSC's executive body is responsible for the organization, maintenance, and accuracy of the company's accounting (financial) records and its annual report. The accuracy of information included in a company's annual report and annual financial statements must also be certified by the company's internal auditor or an audit commission not related through property interests with the company or its shareholders (participants). The general shareholders' meeting (participants') must approve the company's annual reports.

[94] An LLC may and a JSC is obliged to engage an independent external auditor to conduct an audit of annual reports and annual financial statements of the company. The choice of external auditor must be approved by the general shareholders' (participants') meeting.

[95] Most LLCs and JSCs employ an individual with the title of 'Chief Accountant' to be responsible for the establishment of the company's accounting policies, the maintenance of accounting records, and the preparation and submission of finan cial reports. A chief accountant is under the direct supervision of the executive body. Although a company's general director generally has the right to act on behalf of and to bind the company, all financial-related documents of a company also require the signature of the company's chief accountant in order to be valid.

[96] Both LLCs and JSCs are obliged to make public announcements in official specialized sources (i.e., in the journal *Vestnik gosudarstvennoy registratsii*).

[97] A JSC is also required to make announcements in the following cases:

- if at the end of the third, sixth, ninth or twelfth month following the second reporting year (and each subsequent year) a JSC's net asset value turns out to be less than its charter capital by more than 25%;
- if a JSC's board of directors (supervisory board) fails to appoint a new executive body at two subsequent meetings or within two calendar months from the date of termination of powers of the previous sole executive body;
- if a JSC's charter specifies a printed source or an Internet web-page for publishing information intended for its shareholders, the JSC must publish in such sources: (i) announcements on convocation of the general shareholders' meetings (the charter of a JSC with more than 500 shareholders may also specify a specific print media for publishing ballot forms); (ii) information on the JSC's receipt of a MTO or voluntary tender offer (VTO), as well as directors' recommendations regarding the received offer; and (iii) notifications on the possibility to exercise pre-emptive rights to acquire additional newly issued shares of the company.

[98] JSCs also have to disclose certain information related to issuing shares: (i) information on the issue (additional issue) of securities; (ii) information presented in the form of a securities prospectus; (iii) the issuer's consolidated financial statements; (iv) the issuer's quarterly reports; (v) information on the material facts in the issuer's activity; and (vi) other information on the issuer's fulfilment of its obligations and establishment of rights under the offered securities (or securities to be offered).

[99] Information subject to publication under Russian law (including notices on liquidation, reorganization, charter capital change, appointment or dismissal of the general director, address change, etc.) also be disclosed on the publicly available internet site http://fedresurs.ru/. Particular information on bankruptcy proceedings is disclosed on https://bankrot.fedresurs.ru/. Certain information is communicated to the databases by the Tax Authorities; however, legal entities are also required to keep these databases updated. General directors of legal entities that fail to communicate the required information to the federal electronic register can be fined up to RUB10 000 (equal to approx. USD160); subsequent failure is punishable by an increased fine of up to RUB50 000 (approx. USD770).

2.14 Protection of Minority Participants/Shareholders

[100] Russian law provides multiple ways to protect the rights of minority participants/shareholders, among which the most important are listed below.

[101] Information rights – i.e., rights to receive certain information and documents relating to the company's activities. While all minority participants/shareholders have a right to receive information and documents necessary for voting at GPM/GSM, internal regulations of the company, documents evidencing the company's title to its assets, etc., in a JSC accounting documents and minutes of the meeting of collegial executive bodies may be provided only to the shareholders holding at least 25% of voting shares.[17]

[102] Right to sue the management – i.e., rights to claim compensation of losses caused to the company by the members of the supervisory board, collegial and sole executive bodies. While in LLCs any participant may file such a claim, in JSCs this claim may be filed only by the shareholders holding at least 1% of ordinary shares.[18]

[103] Rights to control transactions with the parent company, management, and their affiliates in order to prevent asset dilution – i.e., right to block approval of interested party transactions in certain cases (if such approval requires a decision of the GPM/GSM, whereby the approval is granted by the majority of votes of all non-interested participants/shareholders[19]) or challenge interested party transactions if such transactions were concluded without proper approval.[20]

[104] Right to veto certain decisions of the GPM/GSM – i.e., right to block certain decisions of the GPM/GSM. In a JSC such decisions would include, *inter alia*, amendment of the charter, reorganization and liquidation of the company, placement of new shares in a closed subscription, etc., requiring a 25%+1 voting share to block such decisions; amendment of the charter limiting the rights of holders of preferred shares of a certain type, requiring a 25%+1 voting share of the holders of shares whose rights are not limited and a 25%+1 voting share of the holders of shares whose rights are limited to block such decision. In an LLC such decisions would include amending of the charter, increase of the charter capital by all of the participants, making contributions to the company's assets, etc., and would require more than a one-third participatory interest to block such decisions.

[105] Right to require a buyback of participatory shares/shares – i.e., *in a JSC*: right of holders of voting shares to require the buyback by the company of their shares, for example, in cases of reorganization of the company or the company's conclusion of a major transaction, or amending the charter if such amendments limit their rights and they voted against such decisions or did not participate in voting;[21]

[17] Article 91 of the JSC Law.

[18] Article 71(5) of the JSC Law.

[19] Article 45(3) of the LLC Law, Art. 83(4) of the JSC Law.

[20] Article 45(5) of the LLC Law, Art. 84 of the JSC Law.

[21] Article 75(1) of the JSC Law.

in an LLC: rights of participants to require the company's buyback of participatory shares, for example, when the GPM adopted decisions to enter into a major transaction or increase the charter capital and the participant voted against such decision or did not participate in the voting.[22]

[106] *Only in LLCs and non-public JSCs*: right to demand the expulsion of other participants/shareholders – i.e., right to require through court order the expulsion of other participants/shareholders whose action or failure to act has caused material losses to the company or significantly impedes the company's operations or prevents the company from achieving its goals, including as a result of such participant's/shareholder's gross violation of its obligations set out in the law or the charter.[23] In an LLC, such right is granted to the participants holding at least a 10% participatory interest.[24]

[107] *Only in LLCs*: right to exit from the company – i.e., right to withdraw from the LLC at any time if the charter provides for such withdrawal right,[25] irrespective of the consent of other participants or the LLC itself.

[108] *Only in public JSCs*: right to require the acquisition of shares as a result of a MTO or VTO, i.e., the right to require a shareholder who has become the owner (individually or together with its affiliated persons) of more than 95% of the voting shares in the company (as a result of a mandatory or voluntary offer) to buy out the stakes of the remaining shareholders.[26]

[109] Various protections that may be granted to minority participant/shareholder under the corporate agreement (put options, tag-along right, special rights of the participant, etc.).

2.15 Ways to Acquire a Business in Russia

[110] Russian law differentiates between the following types of business assets relevant for M&A purposes:

- shares in a joint stock company or participatory interests in a limited liability company (share sale and purchase);
- assets of the target company, e.g., all fixed and movable assets (asset sale and purchase);
- 'enterprise' or business as a going concern (called an 'enterprise' under Russian law).

[22] Article 23(2) of the LLC Law.
[23] Article 67(1) of the Civil Code, para. 35 of the Resolution of the Plenum of the Russian Supreme Court dated 23 June 2015, No. 25.
[24] Article 10 of the LLC Law.
[25] Article 94(1) of the Civil Code, Art. 26(1) of the LLC Law.
[26] Article 84.7 of the JSC Law.

2.16 Share Sale Versus Asset Sale

[111] The sale and purchase of shares/participatory interests is a direct transaction between a current shareholder/participant and a purchaser of shares/participatory interests. In such share sale and purchase transaction, the ownership title to the shares/participatory interests is transferred to the purchaser without any impact on the target legal entity.

[112] The academic distinction between a share sale and an asset sale is that in a sale of shares or participatory interests the rights, obligations and risks relating to the legal entity stay with the legal entity and the new owner of the shares bears the costs of any risks.

[113] Since the target of any M&A transaction is either the assets or a license held by the target company, the purchaser may choose another option to gain control over the target and to acquire the assets rather than the legal entity owning such assets.

[114] Acquisition of business by way of acquisition of assets may appear preferable to the purchaser because the existing obligations (such as accounts payable) and risks (such as overdue taxes) of the legal entity do not pass to the purchaser unless such obligations constitute encumbrances on the assets being sold.

[115] However, when considering an asset sale and purchase structure, the following considerations need to be taken into account:

- 20% value added tax (VAT) is payable on the value of the assets transferred (in Russia VAT is not imposed on the transfer of shares);
- the purchaser has to re-apply for licenses/certificates and permits, as those are issued in the name of specific legal entity and may not be assigned from the seller to the purchaser;
- the transfer of title to each real estate object must be registered separately, which can be a cumbersome process (there may be several hundred such objects in a large industrial plant); the agreement on sale of real estate must be governed by Russian law;
- separate agreements need to be signed and registered for the assignment of trademarks, licenses and other intellectual property (IP);
- unlike some jurisdictions, Russia does not have any regime for the automatic transfer of employees in conjunction with a business sale structured as a sale of assets. As such, it is necessary to rehire the personnel or actively transfer the employment agreements of the employees, which requires their cooperation;
- the risk that the asset sale transaction may be invalidated if bankruptcy proceedings are initiated in relation to the seller within six months following the sale;
- a potential risk that a transfer of a substantial number of the assets of a business can be recognized by the court as a sale and purchase of an enterprise and, as a result, the liabilities of that business will pass to the purchaser; and
- the agreement in relation to the sale of immovable assets must be governed by Russian law.

As a result, acquisitions of business by way of acquisition of assets are rare in Russia.

2.17 Sale and Purchase of an Enterprise

[116] The Civil Code defines an enterprise as a combination of assets, IP rights and other rights and obligations used for the purpose of carrying on a business. An enterprise is considered as an immovable asset and is required to be registered with the relevant state authority in the Unified State Register of Immovable Property. Enterprise does not have its corporate identity but is a type of an asset, which has a separate balance sheet.

[117] The agreement in relation to the sale of an enterprise must be governed by Russian law and transfer of title must be registered in the same manner as transfer of title under agreements for the sale of real estate.

[118] Upon the transfer of an enterprise, all assets, rights, and obligations forming a part of it pass to the purchaser, with the exception of licenses, certificates, and other governmental permits for which the new owner of the enterprise must apply separately. Another disadvantage of the sale of an enterprise is that VAT is payable on its transfer.

[119] Given the above, in the Russian M&A market sale of enterprise is extremely rare.

2.18 Mergers Versus Purchase of Shares

[120] M&A transactions may either be in the form of sale and purchase deals as discussed above or accomplished through reorganization.[27] Businesses may be joined through mergers or accessions.

[121] Decisions to merge legal entities (either in the form of merger or accession) may only be made by JSC general shareholders meeting or LLC general participants meeting.

[122] *A merger ('sliyanie')* is the creation of a new company through the transfer of all the rights and obligations of two or more companies that then cease to exist.

[123] In JSCs, a merger starts with the board of directors, which initiates the merger and prepares the agreement for consolidation for further approval by the general shareholders meeting. Shareholders of a merging JSC company must

[27] Russian law (Art. 57(1) of the Civil Code) recognizes five types of corporate reorganization: (i) merger; (ii) accession; (iii) division; (iv) spin-off; and (v) transformation. Merger and accession are aimed at creating a single legal entity, whereas division and spin-off are used to separate businesses and partners. In the course of transformation, a legal entity may change its legal form (a JSC may be transformed into an LLC and vice versa). Upon transformation, all of the rights and obligations of the transformed legal entity are transferred to the new company.

approve the agreement for consolidation by three-fourths of the voting shares of the shareholders present at the meeting, prepare a transfer act in respect of the assets being contributed to the newly created legal entity, approve the transfer act, elect the board of directors of the new company and approve its charter.

[124] Participants of a merging LLC must unanimously make similar decisions except for the election of members of the board of directors, which is not mandatory for an LLC. Participants of a newly created LLC must then elect the executive officers of the LLC.

[125] *An accession ('prisoedinenie')* is the termination of one or more companies by the transfer of all its/their rights and obligations to another company. The acceding legal entities cease to exist following the accession.

[126] The accession procedure of JSCs starts with the board of directors, which submits a decision on reorganization in the form of accession for approval by the shareholders of each legal entity participating in the reorganization. The shareholders of the entity to which another is acceding must approve the accession and the accession agreement by three-fourths of the voting shares of the shareholders present at the meeting, and make other decisions specified in the accession agreement. The shareholders of the acceding JSC have to approve the accession agreement and transfer act.

[127] The scope of decisions to be made by participants of merging LLCs also depends on whether a company is an acceding company or the one to which another legal entity is acceding. Participants of each LLC participating in the accession must make a unanimous decision on accession and approve the accession agreement. The acceding LLC's participants also have to approve the transfer act.

[128] The joint participants' meeting of the new LLC has to amend the charter of the legal entity to which another entity is acceding according to the amendments listed in the accession agreement and also elect the management bodies.

[129] To protect the creditors of the legal entities participating in reorganization, Russian law requires public announcement of the reorganization. In every type of reorganization (any type of merger and accession or transformation), the Tax Authorities must be notified in writing about the commencement of the reorganization. The Tax Authorities enter the relevant information into the Companies' Register, which is also disclosed on the website http://fedresurs.ru/. Once information on the reorganization is entered in the Companies' Register, each legal entity participating in reorganization has to publish an announcement on its reorganization in special mass media sources. The announcement must include details on the reorganization, the procedure for submitting claims by creditors, etc. The creditors of the company have the right to require, within thirty days from the second publication, early repayment of their contractual claims against the company.

2.19 Friendly Versus Hostile Transactions

[130] Currently, the majority of M&A transactions in the Russian market are friendly deals, often preceded by lengthy negotiations between an investor and the selling shareholder(s).

[131] Traditionally, 'hostile takeover' relates to the acquisition of public companies. In Russia, however, there are almost no 'pure' public companies. Despite the fact that many Russian companies are incorporated in the form of a public JSC (including the blue chip companies such as Aeroflot, Gazprom, Rosneft, Lukoil, VTB Bank, and many others) and have certain amounts of shares traded publicly, their majority stakes are not listed. They are either state-owned or belong to private investors and their boards are heavily influenced by the majority shareholders.

3 PRE-CONTRACTUAL PHASE

3.1 Negotiation Process: Statutory Requirements

[132] Among other amendments, a new Article 434.1 (*Negotiations on Conclusion of Agreements*, has been introduced into the Civil Code.

[133] Similar to many other European jurisdictions, Russian Civil Code regulates the pre-contractual behaviour of the parties, in particular, it establishes:

- a statutory duty of the parties to negotiate in good faith[28] when entering into, and in the course of, pre-contractual negotiations;
- a statutory duty of the parties not to disclose or use improperly for their own purposes confidential information in the course of pre-contractual negotiations (i.e., a statutory duty of confidentiality);
- a statutory duty of disclosure of all information material to the transaction; and
- a possibility of the parties entering into an agreement on negotiations, whereby the parties may, among other things, agree on specific criteria that would define good faith behaviour, determine the liability connected with the obligation to negotiate in good faith,[29] etc.

---

[28] The core of the good faith concept is not defined in Art. 434.1 of the Civil Code. However, a common approach to understanding the concept of good faith was established in 2013 in Art. 307 (Definition of Obligation) of the Civil Code. Under Art. 307, when establishing, performing and terminating -obligations the parties should: (i) take into account their mutual rights and legitimate interests; (ii) mutually provide any assistance required in order to achieve the purpose of the obligations; and (iii) provide each other with all the necessary information.

[29] For further information regarding the '*Agreement on Negotiations*', *see* the 'Preliminary Documentation' section below.

3.2 Statutory Duty to Negotiate in Good Faith

[134] As noted above, Russian law[30] expressly requires the parties to negotiate in good faith. The concept of good faith in relation to pre-contractual negotiations means that the parties may not enter into or proceed with negotiations without an intention to enter into an agreement (e.g., by entering into negotiations solely to solicit commercially sensitive information from the other party or to prevent the conclusion of an agreement with a third party[31]).

[135] Article 434.1[32] further provides that the following actions are examples of bad faith:

- provision to the other party of incomplete and false information and/or failure to provide information which, in view of the nature of the agreement being negotiated, should be provided to the other party;
- unexpected and unjustified withdrawal from the negotiations where the other party could not have reasonably expected such withdrawal.

[136] If a dispute arises whether there was a breach of a duty to negotiate in good faith in circumstances listed above, the burden of proof is on the party that committed such actions. In other situations, it is the obligation of the claimant to prove that there was breach of a duty to negotiate in good faith by the other party.

[137] Pursuant to Article 434.1, a party that acted in bad faith may be ordered to pay damages comprised of:

(a) the costs incurred by the non-defaulting party in connection with carrying on the negotiations (legal and other costs); and
(b) the losses incurred in connection with the loss of the opportunity to enter into a transaction with a third party.

In addition to the statutory liability listed above, the parties may agree by contract that penalties in agreed amount should be payable for breach of requirement to negotiate in good faith.

[138] While the scope of damages falling under item (a) is uncontroversial, the Civil Code does not contain any calculation method for determining the amount of damage incurred due to the loss of the opportunity to enter into an agreement with a third party (as set out in item (b) above). As such, the recoverable losses may be calculated similar to the loss of profit.

30 Article 434.1 of the Civil Code.

31 Article 19 of the Resolution of the Plenum of the Supreme Court of the Russian Federation No. 7 'On Application by the Courts of Certain Provisions of the Civil Code Relating to Contractual Liability', dated 24 March 2016, further clarifies this issue.

32 Article 434.1(2) of the Civil Code.

[139] The Supreme Court of the Russian Federation has further clarified[33] that a party conducting negotiations in bad faith should pay damages in the amount to restore the aggrieved party to the position that it would have been in if the negotiations had not occurred. However, the Supreme Court has not specified what is recoverable by way of costs incurred in connection with the loss of opportunity to enter into a transaction with a third party.. –There was one case where the landlord was awarded lost income that resulted from unexpected withdrawal from negotiations by the potential tenant.[34]

[140] Liability for bad faith conduct (including a seller's failure to disclose material information and a purchaser's breach of its duty of confidentiality) may be established even after the transaction has closed (or the agreement has been entered into). A negotiating party is liable for the bad faith conduct of all its employees and not only those specifically authorized to conduct the negotiations on its behalf.

3.3 Statutory Duty of Disclosure

[141] In accordance with Article 434.1 of the Civil Code, the provision by one party in negotiations to the other party of incomplete or false information and/or failure to provide information which, in view of the nature of the contemplated contract should be provided to the other party, is considered to be bad faith conduct.

[142] Damages for breach of the statutory duty of disclosure are the same as for breach of the duty to negotiate in good faith, and comprise compensation for: (i) negotiation costs; and (ii) losses from the loss of an opportunity to enter into a transaction with a third party.

[143] In addition, if a negotiated agreement is entered into on the basis of incomplete or false information (or in the absence of information which, in view of the nature of the agreement, should have been provided to the other party), the aggrieved party can sue the offending party in court for damages or for invalidation of the agreement.[35]

[144] A party can claim that a transaction is invalid with reference to Article 178 (invalidity of transactions entered into under the influence of material misunderstanding) or Article 179 (invalidity of transactions entered into under the influence of fraud, violence, threat or adverse circumstances) of the Civil Code.

---

[33] Article 20 of the Resolution of the Plenum of the Supreme Court of the Russian Federation No. 7 'On Application by the Courts of Certain Provisions of the Civil Code Relating to Contractual Liability', dated 24 March 2016.

[34] Decision on the Moscow Arbitration Court on case No. 41-90214/2016 of 29 November 2017.

[35] Article 21 of the Resolution of the Plenum of the Supreme Court of the Russian Federation No. 7 'On Application by the Courts of Certain Provisions of the Civil Code Relating to Contractual Liability', dated 24 March 2016.

3.4 Statutory Duty of Confidentiality

[145] Article 434.1 of the Civil Code determines the requirements applicable in respect of the receipt of confidential information in the context of negotiations. In particular, it establishes that a party receiving information identified as 'confidential'[36] in the course of negotiations may not (irrespective of whether a final agreement is entered into or not):

- disclose such information; or
- use such information improperly for its own purposes.

[146] Pursuant to Article 434.1, if a party to negotiations provides confidential information to the other party and such other party uses it improperly for its own purposes or discloses such information to third parties, the latter is considered to have acted in bad faith and may be required to pay damages to the disclosing party (although Article 434.1 does not give any guidance as to how these damages should be calculated).

[147] Also, the statutory duty of confidentiality in negotiations is applicable even if the parties do not enter into a separate confidentiality agreement.

3.5 Pre-contractual Documentation

[148] Typical pre-contractual documentation seen in the Russian M&A market includes the following:

- confidentiality agreement;
- letter of intent (memorandum of understanding, term sheet or heads of terms);
- agreement on negotiations; and/or
- exclusivity agreement.

In a situation where the parties are willing to enter into a 'binding termsheet', they can enter into so-called preliminary agreement under which the parties agree to negotiate and enter into a contract in the future.

[149] It should be noted that entering into a confidentiality agreement, agreement on negotiations, memorandum of understanding and exclusivity agreement in the form of separate documents is not required. As a matter of generally accepted practice, the provisions of all four of these agreements are included in one document, such as a letter of intent or a term sheet, whereby the parties may specifically indicate that provisions relating to confidentiality, exclusivity and the negotiations procedures are legally binding.

[36] For further information regarding 'Confidential Information', *see* the 'Confidentiality Agreement' section below.

3.6 Confidentiality Agreement

[150] Confidentiality agreements generally prohibit unauthorized disclosure of confidential information. Russian law expressly grants statutory protection only to certain types of information (e.g., state or commercial secrets, banking secrecy).

[151] However, statutory duty of confidentiality[37] (in relation to negotiations and possibility of the parties to enter into an agreement on negotiations), which may provide for additional rights and obligations of the parties related to good faith negotiations, increases the chances of enforcement.

[152] As the general rule, the confidentiality agreements concluded in the Russian market contain the following key provisions:

- restrictions on the scope of use of the confidential information by employees and consultants of the receiving party (i.e., use of the obtained confidential information solely for the purpose of evaluating the contemplated transaction);
- permitted disclosure of confidential information to third parties (e.g., disclosure of confidential information at the request of state authorities, or in order to comply with the stock exchange requirements);
- measure of damages for breach of the confidentiality obligations;
- provisions requiring the return and/or destruction of the disclosed confidential information;
- non-solicitation/no contact with employees or customers of the party disclosing the information; and
- a prohibition on announcements with respect to the proposed transaction.

[153] A confidentiality agreement is commonly entered into at the initial stages of the transaction, and commonly has a term of up to three years.

[154] Under Russian law, it is difficult for parties to prove damage arising from a breach of a confidentiality agreement since the disclosing party must prove: (i) the fact that the information was disclosed by the receiving party in breach of the agreement; (ii) the actual damage suffered by the disclosing party and the amount of such damage; and (iii) the cause-and-effect relationship between the breach of the agreement and the incurred damage.

[155] Another remedy available for breach of confidentiality obligations is a court order (injunction) preventing disclosure of the confidential information. For example, an injunction may be available as an interim remedy for a claimant seeking damages for breach of the confidentiality obligations if the ongoing disclosure of information would cause him further harm.

[37] As noted above in the 'Negotiation Process' section, the new Art. 434.1 of the Civil Code provides that if a party receives confidential information in the course of negotiations, the recipient must not disclose such information to third parties or use it for its own purpose, irrespective of whether the negotiated agreement will be entered into following the negotiations. The party in breach of such statutory duty of confidentiality must pay the other party's damages.

3.7 Letter of Intent

[156] It is common in the Russian market for the parties to enter into a preliminary document described as a letter of intent, memorandum of understanding, heads of agreement or term sheet. (The choice of description for such a document is largely a matter of practical preference; the substance of the document is similar in each case.) The main function of the document is to facilitate negotiations by outlining the principal parameters and timing of the proposed transaction, usually in a non-binding form. It may also contain a limited number of legally binding terms, such as provisions regarding the conduct of negotiations, confidentiality and/or exclusivity.

[157] A letter of intent commonly records the following matters:

- the identity of the target company or the group of target companies covered by the deal;
- the shares/participatory interests to be acquired;
- the purchase price (as a fixed price or as a price range) or approach to the determination of the purchase price;
- the deadlines for completing due diligence and other transaction steps; and
- the deadlines for the execution of the transaction documents.

[158] It should be noted that, under Russian law, there is a risk that a letter of intent could be construed as a binding agreement or a preliminary agreement within the meaning of Russian law, being a legally binding agreement under which the parties can use the courts to enforce the execution of the main agreement (preliminary agreements are discussed further below). For this reason, if the intention is that the letter of intent should *not* create a legally binding obligation to conclude a transaction, it should contain an express statement to that effect.

3.8 Preliminary Agreement ('Binding Termsheet')

[159] Under the Russian Civil Code, a preliminary agreement is a special form of pre-transactional document under which the parties undertake to enter into a binding agreement (so-called main agreement) at a future date. Specifically, Article 429 of the Civil Code provides that the parties to a preliminary agreement undertake to enter into a binding agreement in the future for the transfer of property, performance of work or the provision of services on the terms and conditions provided in the preliminary agreement. In substance, therefore, a preliminary agreement within the meaning of Russian law has a nature of a 'binding termsheet'.

[160] The preliminary agreement must contain sufficiently detailed terms to define the subject matter of the main agreement, as well as any terms which a party requested to agree upon at the time of concluding the preliminary agreement. If the parties subsequently fail to reach agreement on aspects of the terms of the transaction that are not considered to be material under Russian law, courts can determine those terms and treat the main agreement as having been concluded on the terms determined by the court.

[161] The preliminary agreement should specify a period of time within which the main agreement must be entered into. If such a period of time is not agreed in the preliminary agreement, the main agreement must be entered into within one year from the date of the preliminary agreement. A party may request a court to compel the other party to enter into the main agreement within six months from the day of the breach of the other party's obligation to enter into the main agreement. If neither of the parties requests that the main agreement be entered into within the period of time specified in the preliminary agreement, the preliminary agreement will terminate.

[162] The obligations of the parties to the preliminary agreement may be secured with a pledge or penalty may be agreed to be payable in the case of a breach by a party.

[163] In general, preliminary agreements are rarely concluded in practice. The parties in M&A transactions normally sign a non-binding letter of intent at an early stage when the full terms of the transaction have not yet been negotiated, and therefore do not want to be bound at that point in time.

3.9 Agreement on Negotiations

[164] The Civil Code now expressly allows the parties to enter into an agreement on negotiations[38] whereby the parties may set out requirements regarding the negotiation process. Such agreement may contain provisions on:

- the criteria for good/bad faith negotiations;
- responsibility for the parties' negotiation costs;
- other similar rights and obligations of the parties; and
- penalty for breach of agreement on negotiations.

[165] Article 434.1 of the Civil Code expressly provides that an agreement on negotiations may not exclude or limit the liability of a party for bad faith conduct of negotiations.

3.10 Exclusivity Agreement

[166] The main purpose of a typical exclusivity agreement in an M&A transaction is to prevent the seller from offering the shares to third parties during the agreed exclusivity period.

[167] As a general rule, the principal terms of an exclusivity agreement are as follows:

[38] Article 434.1(5) of the Civil Code.

- no entry into negotiations with any third parties in respect of the sale of all or part of a business or a disposal of material assets of the target;
- an obligation to ensure that members of the seller's group and the seller's employees, directors and representatives comply with the exclusivity obligation; and
- no disclosure to third parties of information in connection with the sale of the business.

[168] The typical exclusivity period is two to three months. Normally, the period of exclusivity is the period of time that the parties estimate will be required in order for the purchaser to complete its due diligence of the target and for the parties to finalize negotiations of the transaction documents.

[169] There is a debate about what would be typical remedies for breach of the exclusivity agreement – in Russian practice those would be: court injunction, compensation of costs, and, if the parties agreed so in the agreement on negotiations, penalty and/or compensation of lost opportunity.

4 DUE DILIGENCE PROCESS

4.1 Scope of Legal Due Diligence

[170] The buyer and its advisers will prepare a list of questions and requests for information to elicit from the seller sufficient information to enable the buyer to gain as complete an understanding of a target company as possible. The successful performance of a due diligence review depends on understanding what the buyer is evaluating and why. The buyer and its advisers should tailor the information request accordingly.

[171] A full legal due diligence review covers corporate, finance, regulatory, real estate, employment, commercial, IP and litigation issues. Environmental audits are carried out only in relation to the target companies operating in specific industries, such as natural resources extraction, production, construction.

[172] The following matters are usually examined in relation to the target company:

(a) proper establishment of the company;
(b) proper issuance of the company's shares;
(c) the seller's title to the shares and encumbrances on the shares;
(d) composition of the company's shareholders and any agreements governing their relations;
(e) matters of company management and target company structure;
(f) the company's participation in other companies;
(g) the company's title to its assets, real estate and movable property;
(h) the company's rights to IP, trademarks, patents and the like;

(i) availability of licenses/permits for the company's operations;
(j) the company's client base (in particular, material and long-term contracts);
(k) the company's material obligations;
(l) third party debts owed to the company;
(m) insurance matters;
(n) employment matters (including the company's employment agreements, including agreements with the top managers);
(o) environmental protection matters; and
(p) litigation involving the company and its audits and inspections by government authorities.

4.2 Setting Up and Operating a Data Room/Virtual Data Room

[173] For conducting a due diligence, the seller either delivers copies of the documents requested by the buyer to the buyer's consultants or makes them available in a data room. Unless the legislation regulating a target's activities imposes certain restrictions (e.g., bank secrecy restrictions) and requires documents to be provided to third parties for review only in physical data rooms, most companies prefer to set up online transaction portals called 'virtual data rooms' (VDRs), especially when a project involves the due diligence of several companies located in different regions or countries.

[174] The preparation of a data room usually starts with the appointment of a team responsible for collating all the information to be made available in the data room. For VDRs, a site manager(s)/administrator(s) should also be appointed to monitor and control technical operation of the site.

[175] In the course of initial preparation of the data room, it is advisable to categorize all documents into folders and sub-folders and maintain an index of them. New documents should then be filed in a supplemental index (the headings of which should mirror those in the main index) in the order in which they are received.

[176] Before submission the seller should check that all documents are complete, e.g., all pages, including schedules, are attached. Copies of agreements should, where appropriate, be copies which are fully signed and dated; spreadsheets or other lists of information should specify the date as of which the information has been provided. Copies of original documents (or the originals themselves) should be submitted and, in the case of an online data room, sent to the online data room service provider for scanning onto the site. All paper documents should be sent in a clean state (e.g., loose leaf and no tags or post-it notes).

[177] It is necessary to decide whether copying, printing or downloading will be permitted and, if so, whether this will apply to individual documents or certain categories of documents, for example, accounts, on a section or document basis.

[178] From the seller's side perspective, the release of information requires careful planning. During the initial phase of the due diligence, it may be advisable to limit the documents disclosed to generic information relating to the target business and its customers.

4.3 Information Requests/Q&As

[179] As the due diligence exercise progresses, and the buyer learns more about a target company, the buyer should make further, more specific information requests. For both parties, it is very important to consider how to handle and streamline such supplemental requests.

[180] In the case of a VDR, it is common to require all information requests and responses to be submitted via the Q&A function of the site. Each party may assign a point of contact who will ask/respond to all questions through the Q&A function.

[181] The buyer should indicate the level of priority of each request, which will help the seller's transaction team focus on answering the questions which the buyer considers more essential to the proposed transaction.

[182] A master spreadsheet of Q&As submitted should be maintained and used to monitor the seller's response to all of the matters set out in an information request. To the extent that the seller has not answered a request, or the seller's response is not satisfactory, or the disclosed documentation raises an issue, the buyer should be able to ask further questions.

[183] It is advisable to consider the optimal manner of dealing with information requests. Options may include: (i) referring to a document (or part of a document) already provided in the data room; (ii) providing an additional document to the data room; and (iii) drafting a short response, such as a paragraph which summarizes the key points relating to the relevant issue. Both parties should hold their own team meetings on a regular basis during the period for which the data room is opened to consider how to improve the Q&A process.

4.4 Due Diligence Reports: Local Practice

[184] The format of the legal due diligence report will vary depending upon the buyer's instructions, the proposed scope and the time available. Typically, a legal due diligence report contains the following information:

- a summary of material legal issues arising from the due diligence review;
- areas where the quality or lack of the information is considered an issue;
- recommendations for resolving risks or protecting (contractually or otherwise) the buyer from the risks identified upon the due diligence review;
- a list of the information the seller has made available for review; and
- limitations, assumptions and qualifications based on which the report has been prepared.

[185] In the meantime, in the Russian market buyers typically instruct their legal adviser to report on a 'red flag' basis, highlighting only those legal issues that the legal adviser has identified that may be material in the context of a proposed transaction for which the due diligence is carried out.

4.5 Information Available Publicly

[186] Public searches on a target company may be an important source of information, such as:

- the official website of the Federal Tax Service and the journal '*Vestnik gosudarstvennoy registratsii*' contains information about the current corporate status of the target, in particular the registered information about the target's bankruptcy, reorganization or liquidation;
- the Federal Tax Service is obliged to provide a copy of the Charter of the company to any interested person;
- the official website of the Federal Service for Intellectual Property contains information about the target's IP rights;
- the online database of the Russian state arbitration courts contains information about current commercial disputes involving the target; and
- the Unified Register of Immovable Property contains information ownership and lease rights to immovable properties (provided that the lease is executed for a term of at least one year) as well as certain encumbrances and limitations.

In addition, it should be noted that pubic companies are obliged to disclose significant amount of information on their corporate websites and a specially dedicated website.

4.6 Issues of Confidentiality/Third Party Confidentiality

[187] Confidentiality issues arise at various stages of the M&A transaction process, but most commonly at the due diligence phase. Therefore, before providing the buyer with access to any information, the starting point of the due diligence process should be the requirement to enter into a confidentiality agreement containing the customary restrictions, such as a prohibition on the buyer approaching any of the target group's customers without the seller's prior written consent.

[188] The seller also needs to develop the data room rules and make sure the buyer signs a copy of the rules. The data room rules govern the use of the data room, set out the Q&A process and impose the duty of confidentiality on each person entering the data room or using the online site (as appropriate) in accordance with the terms of a separate confidentiality agreement, which usually will have already been executed.

[189] Before placing documents in the data room, the seller may consider redacting certain sensitive information from them. Redaction commonly involves removing:

- commercial terms or information, such as fees or pricing;
- documents which contain confidentiality provisions which prevent their disclosure without the counterparty's consent; and
- personal data information.

[190] The seller should appoint a member of the transaction team to review documents before they are submitted to the data room.

[191] Generally, unless an agreement containing a confidentiality undertaking expressly permits disclosure in a due diligence process, any disclosure of confidential information will be a breach of the agreement. In order to mitigate or manage the potential legal consequences of breach of a confidentiality undertaking, a number of measures can be taken (e.g., trying to obtain third parties' consent prior to the disclosure, where the target's relationships with such persons allow it).

[192] The general Russian law principle of freedom of information provides that distribution of information may not be restricted unless otherwise provided by law. It is possible to establish a 'commercial secret' regime with respect to the information that a party wishes to keep confidential. Information which is considered to be a 'commercial secret' under Russian law enjoys statutory protection. Commercial secrets, including know-how, comprise scientific, technical, technological, production-related, financial, economic or other information, including production-related secrets:

- that have actual or potential commercial value because they are unknown to third parties;
- that are not freely accessible on legitimate grounds; and
- to which their owner has applied the status of a commercial secret (i.e., the owner takes certain measures to protect the confidentiality of the information constituting a commercial secret).

[193] Whether or not the commercial secret regime applies is at the discretion (and depends on the actions) of the owner of the information. Under Russian law, in order to establish that the commercial secret regime does apply to certain information, the owner of such information must: (i) list the information which is considered confidential; (ii) limit access to such information by setting up a special procedure for handling the information and controlling compliance with the procedure; (iii) keep a record of all persons who have access to such information; (iv) regulate the use of such information by employees under their employment contracts and by third parties under civil (commercial) law contracts; and (v) affix a 'commercial secret' stamp to documents that contain confidential information. If the information owner fails to undertake any of the above actions, it may be argued that the information should not enjoy the statutory protection granted to commercial secrets.

4.7 Data Protection

[194] In the course of providing any information, the seller should ensure that the disclosure of such information will not constitute a breach of applicable legislation, for example, personal data or banking secrecy protection requirements. The seller has to consult with its legal counsel (internal or external) before making any disclosure. At a minimum, it is important to ensure that:

- the members of the transaction teams are aware of their data protection responsibilities;
- all persons to whom the information is disclosed have entered into confidentiality agreements and been prevented from using the information for any purposes other than the transaction;
- appropriate practical safeguards are in place to ensure the security of information disclosed (e.g., through the use of a data room governed by appropriate data room rules, as discussed above).

[195] Both parties should control access to the data room and supervise its use in accordance with the rules agreed at the initial stage. If the seller sets up its data room through a third party, such third party should also be required to put in place appropriate measures to prevent the unauthorized or unlawful processing of the information with restricted access.

5 SHARE PURCHASE: CONTRACTUAL STRUCTURING

[196] M&A transactions in the Russian market are structured as an acquisition of shares in the charter capital of a joint stock company or participatory interests in a limited liability company (i.e., share sale and purchase). The standard document formalizing such an acquisition is a share sale and purchase agreement (SPA). Below we describe the key provisions of an SPA under Russian law.

5.1 Purchase Price and Price Adjustment

[197] Russian law does not provide any strict rules in relation to determining price in agreements. The price can be fixed, determined by the formula, or even agreeable in the future. If the price is 'agreeable in the future'[39] and the parties fail to agree, the price may be determined by the court with reference to comparable goods or services (i.e., comparable transactions).

[198] There are no impediments under Russian law to the use of completion accounts mechanism, whether with reference to the level of debt, amount of inventory or both. For the purposes of drafting the completion accounts mechanism it

[39] Article 424 of the Civil Code.

should be taken into account that Russian accounting rules are different from International Financial Reporting Standards (IFRS – also noted that most of the substantial companies prepare their accounts in accordance with both Russian accounting rules and IFRS requirements).

Locked box mechanism is also used in Russian practice, although less frequently and mostly in private equity transactions.

Earn-out structures are also used in practice; however, the 'classic' earn-out structure whereby the seller is entitled to a part of profit of the target for a certain period of time after completion is less and less popular. Many practitioners view options with deferred completion as a type of earn-out.

5.2 Conditions Precedent

[199] Pursuant to Article 327.1, performance of obligations, as well as the exercise, amendment or termination of certain rights under the agreement, may be conditional on the occurrence of certain circumstances set out in the agreement, irrespectively whether a party has control over such circumstances or not.

[200] In Russian M&A practice, commonly encountered conditions precedent include the following:

- obtaining regulatory approvals, such as obtaining prior consent from the Federal Antimonopoly Service of the Russian Federation (FAS) (and/or similar foreign antitrust authorities, where the target, the seller or the purchaser have operations);
- completion of reorganization of the target company in preparation for its sale;
- obtaining licenses (permits, certificates, etc.);
- obtaining corporate approvals of the parties;
- obtaining third party consents or waivers (such as waivers of rights of first refusal and requirements to make tender offers, obtaining creditors' consents and addressing change of control provisions under existing contracts); and
- the seller performing certain actions prior to completion, such as remedying defects identified in the course of a due diligence or disposing of non-core assets.

5.3 Pre-completion Undertakings

[201] Where there is a time interval between the signing and the closing of a transaction, SPAs commonly contain pre-completion undertakings obliging the seller not to take certain actions and to procure that the target company does not take certain actions that might adversely affect the value of the target or its business.

[202] As a matter of Russian law, the management of a company must act in the interests of the company (and, presumably, not in the interests of its shareholders).

As a result, it is questionable whether a shareholder can order the management to refrain from certain actions without the purchaser's prior consent.

[203] Under the provisions regarding corporate agreements, the company's creditors and other third parties may enter into a corporate (shareholders) agreement with the existing shareholders of the company for the purpose of securing their interests (so-called *quasi-corporate agreement*).[40] In particular, a quasi-corporate agreement may require the company's shareholders to exercise their corporate rights in a certain way or to refrain from taking certain actions, for the benefit of company creditors or other third parties. As such, it is possible to impose pre-completion undertakings under Russian law under this regime.

[204] Thus, in an M&A transaction, the purchaser has an opportunity to ensure the protection of its rights between signing and closing by entering into a quasi-corporate agreement with the seller, whereby the selling shareholders accept certain restrictions on exercise of their rights over the target shares in favour of the purchaser.[41] The provisions on quasi-corporate agreements do not explicitly envisage the possibility of the target company itself being a party to such an agreement, and it is therefore questionable whether the target company can itself be bound by pre-completion undertakings.

[205] As a general rule, breach of pre-completion undertakings by the selling shareholder may entitle the purchaser to claim damages and terminate the agreement. The situation may be different where the seller does not have the contractual right to bind the company and the competence of the shareholders meeting does not include the items included in the pre-contractual undertakings.

[206] In addition to claiming damages, pursuant to the new Article 393(6) of the Civil Code, the purchaser is entitled to seek an injunction in court to enforce a pre-completion undertaking. The purchaser can bring such a claim in the event of a real threat of a breach of an existing obligation.

5.4 Completion Mechanics

[207] The list of actions that the parties undertake to perform at completion (in addition to transferring shares or participation interests) is largely transaction-specific in that it depends on the specific terms of the relevant transaction. There are, however, a number of mandatory actions stipulated by Russian law which the parties have to undertake in order to complete the transaction.

[40] Article 67.2(9) of the Civil Code.

[41] It should be noted that the purchaser might incur costs if under a corporate agreement the purchaser acquires the right to determine the actions of the company's shareholders; for example, it may be liable for damage incurred by the target company.

5.5 Completion: Participation Interests in a Russian LLC

[208] The vast majority of commercial legal entities established in Russia are limited liability companies and joint stock companies (joint stock companies are commonly referred to by the Russian abbreviation 'AO' or its English abbreviation 'JSC', and limited liability companies by the Russian abbreviation 'OOO' or its English abbreviation 'LLC').

[209] In LLCs the charter capital is divided into participatory interests (which is a percentage of the nominal ruble value of the participant's ownership interests to the total charter capital). Participatory interests are not deemed to be securities; hence, securities market regulations are not applicable. Each participant has the number of votes corresponding to its participatory interest unless the LLC Law or the company charter provides otherwise.[42]

[210] Title to participation interests in the charter capital of a Russian LLC is treated as having been transferred from the seller to the purchaser at the moment the relevant record of that transfer is made by the state registration authorities[43] in the USRLE).

[211] Under the LLC Law as it currently stands, the purchaser and the seller need to execute the participatory interest purchase agreement in the presence of a notary (i.e., transactions involving the transfer of participatory interests must be notarized (certified by a Russian public notary)). Failure to do so will result in the transaction being invalid.[44]

[212] The notary certifies the participatory interest purchase agreement and, within two business days (or such longer term as is stipulated by the agreement), submits to the registration authorities an application to record the relevant changes in the USRLE.[45] Title to the participation interest transfers to the purchaser from the date on which the relevant entry is made in the USRLE.[46] The procedure for registration of changes in the USRLE takes five business days from the

---

[42] Articles 66(1) and 66.3(3)(para. 5) of the Civil Code; Art. 32(1) of the LLC Law.

[43] The tax authorities are required to maintain the USRLE. The USRLE is the official public database containing information on all legal entities registered in the Russian Federation. The extract from the USRLE issued by the tax authorities is an ultimate evidence of ownership over the participatory interests of the LLC. The details of the LLC's participants and their respective participation interests must also be recorded in the register of participants that is maintained by the LLC itself.

[44] Article 21(11) of Federal Law No. 14-FZ 'On Limited Liability Companies' dated 8 February 1998, lists the statutory requirements of notarial certification of transactions with participatory interests of an limited liability companies (e.g., sale and purchase or pledge of a participatory interests). In the absence of such notarial certification, the transaction is considered invalid.

[45] The relevant application must be signed and stamped by the notary who notarized the transaction (before the amendments, such application was signed directly by representatives of the legal entity selling the participatory interests).

[46] Article 21(12) of the Law on Limited Liability Companies.

date of submission of the application by the notary. The notary is required to provide to the applicant (i.e., the target company) an extract confirming the transfer of the participatory interest within three business days of the registration of the transfer.

[213] As a general rule, the procedure for registration of the transfer of a participatory interest in an LLC takes up to seven business days in total from the moment of notarization of the SPA to the date when the transfer is reflected in the USRLE.

[214] The notarial fee for certification depends on the transaction value. For this purpose, the transaction value is the greater of the agreement value specified by the parties and the nominal value of the participatory interest.[47] The notary fee is calculated according to the following formulae:[48]

- for transactions having a value of up to RUB1 000 000 (approx. USD1 670) – *0.5% of the transaction value, but no* less than RUB1 500 (approx. USD25);
- for transactions having a value from RUB1 000 001 (approx. USD1 670) to RUB10 000 000 (approx. USD167 000) – RUB5 000 (approx. USD80) + 0.5% of the transaction value exceeding RUB1 000 000 (approx. USD1 670); and
- for transactions having a value of RUB10 000 001 (approx. USD167 000) or more – RUB32 000 (approx. USD530) + 0.15% of the transaction value exceeding RUB10 000 000 (approx. USD167 000), subject to a total cap of RUB150 000.

[215] By virtue of law, each participant has the right of first refusal in relation to participatory interests being sold by other participants to a third party. The company itself may have the right of first refusal ('second' refusal versus the participants' right of first refusal) if the charter of the LLC so provides. The default rule is that the other participants may choose to exercise their right of first refusal at the same price at which the relevant participatory interests are being offered to the third party. However, the LLC charter may provide for a different method of calculating the price for the purposes of right of first refusal: (i) a fixed price or (ii) a formula based on certain criteria, e.g., value of net assets of the company, net profit for the previous year. The LLC Law also allows participants to introduce other restrictions on transfers of participatory interests such as consent of the other participants. The selling shareholder's non-compliance with rights of first refusal allows the remaining non-defaulting participants to assume the purchaser's rights in respect of the offered shares within the later of: (i) the date falling three months from the date when the shares were sold in breach of the right of first refusal; or (ii) within three months from the date on which the non-defaulting shareholders became aware of such breach.

[47] Section 1(5) of Art. 333.25 of the Tax Code.

[48] Section 4.1 of Art. 333.24 of the Tax Code.

5.6 Completion: Shares in a Russian Joint Stock Company

[216] The charter capital of a JSC is divided into shares. All shares (ordinary and preferred) of Russian JSCs exist only in non-documentary form, and title to the shares is recorded in the share register (kept in electronic form). The share register of a JSC is required to be maintained by an independent share registrar pursuant to an agreement entered into between the relevant company and the registrar. Shares are deemed to be securities; their initial and each subsequent issuance must be registered with the Central Bank.

[217] Unlike with LLCs, transactions involving shares in a JSC (whether public or non-public) do not require notarial certification, and transfer of title to the shares is recorded by the share register.

[218] In accordance with the Russian Securities Market Law,[49] the transfer of title to JSC shares is deemed to occur when an entry is made in the target company's shareholder register evidencing that the shares are registered in the purchaser's personal account.[50] The entry in the company's shareholder register should be made on the basis of a transfer order[51] instructing the company's registrar to transfer the shares to the purchaser's account.

[219] The statutory period for the registration of a transfer of shares by the share registrar is three business days, but in practice transfers can be registered within a shorter period of time. Under Russian law, the information contained in the shareholder register is conclusive evidence of share ownership, and can be confirmed by an extract from the seller's share account.

[220] It is also possible for shares of a JSC to be held through a depository (if traded publicly on a stock exchange). The right to the shares is registered by an entity performing depositary activity and in such cases the depository appears in the company's shareholder register as the holder of the shares. The shares can then be transferred by way of a transfer from the seller's account to a personal account of the purchaser opened with the same depository, and title to the shares is considered to be transferred from the seller to the purchaser from the moment that an entry is made in the purchaser's personal account reflecting the transfer.[52]

[221] If provided by the charter of a non-public JSC, the shareholders in the non-public JSC have the right of first refusal in relation to shares being sold by the other shareholders to a third party. The price at which the right of first refusal is exercised may be: (i) the price as offered to the third party, (ii) a fixed price specified in

49 Article 29 of Federal Law No. 39-FZ 'On the Securities Market' dated 22 April 1996.

50 The purchaser must open a personal account in the target company's shareholders register prior to completion of the transaction, so that the shares of the target company may be transferred to that account.

51 The form of the transfer order should be obtained from the company's registrar.

52 Article 29 of Federal Law No. 39-FZ 'On the Securities Market' dated 22 April 1996.

the company's charter or (iii) the price calculated on the basis of a formula specified in the company's charter. The charter of a non-public JSC may also give the company a right of first refusal ('second' refusal after the shareholders' right of first refusal). The time for responding to an offer notice is two months from the date of the notice, unless the charter provides for a shorter period of time. The selling shareholder's non-compliance with rights of first refusal allows the purchaser's rights to be assigned to the remaining non-defaulting shareholders. Such rights can be exercised on the later of: (i) the date falling three months from the date when the shares were sold in breach of the right of first refusal; or (ii) within three months from the date on which the non-defaulting shareholders became aware of such breach.

5.7 Escrow Accounts

[222] Escrow arrangements are sometimes used in M&A transactions to ensure that payment is made for transfer of title to shares or to secure deferred payments.

[223] One context in which use of an escrow account may be commercially desirable is the sale of a participation interest in an LLC where, because of the recent changes to the LLC Law (described above), transfer of title to the participatory interest depends on registration in the USRLE, which takes some time after signature of the associated agreement. There is therefore a risk for the purchaser in such a transaction associated with payment of the purchase price at the moment of signing the SPA (i.e., prior to registration of the transfer) and possible refusal by the registration authority to register the transfer.[53] In addition, the seller may be unwilling to assume the risk of committing to the transfer of the participatory interest before receipt of the purchase price.

[224] The Civil Code describes the escrow arrangements are as follows:

- A special escrow account is opened with a bank. The account is designated for holding funds received from the depositor (i.e., the purchaser) for the purposes of their subsequent transfer to the seller upon the satisfaction of certain conditions, as set out in a three-party escrow agreement between the purchaser, the seller and the bank.
- Once the funds have been deposited, neither the purchaser nor the seller can use the escrow funds other than as permitted by the escrow agreement. The bank may not close the escrow account until the expiry of the term of the escrow arrangement unless otherwise provided by the escrow agreement.
- Upon the satisfaction of the escrow release conditions, the bank must release the funds to the seller. If the escrow release conditions are not satisfied before the expiry of the escrow agreement, the funds are required to be returned to the purchaser.

[53] We are aware of cases where the registration authorities refused to register the transfer of title.

5.8 Warranties in Russian Law

[225] When describing the concept of warranties, Russian law uses the term 'representation on circumstances' ('*zavereniya ob obstoyatel'stvah*', Article 431.2 of the Civil Code).

Warranties can be given by a party with respect to itself (e.g., capacity, authority, financial status), the shares (e.g., title, no encumbrances) or the underlying business (e.g., a set of business warranties, including assets, liabilities, licenses and permits). In practice, the scope of the warranties included in a Russia-centric share purchase agreement is no different from the scope of the warranties included in a typical cross-border share purchase agreement.

The warranties may be given by a party to the contract or, as an alternative, a third party with an interest in the contract (typically, by a shareholder or an affiliate of the party).

A party giving the warranties will be liable for its breach if it was aware, or had reasonable grounds to believe, that its counterparty will rely on the warranties. There is a general presumption that the counterparty to a contract will rely on the warranties given in that contract.

In contrast with English law, Russian law does not recognize the concept of repetition (or deemed repetition) of warranties on completion. Under Russian law, the warranties may be given only with respect to the facts existing at the time the contract is signed. In order to achieve the same effect as repetition, the entire set of warranties will usually be re-signed at the time of completion.

One important debate in practice is whether the recipient of the warranties is required to act in good faith when relying on warranties. The courts are generally inclined to take position that the recipient of the warranties must exercise due care when receiving the warranties. By way of example, the courts have denied damages for breach of a warranty relating to the absence of encumbrances over immovable property where information concerning the relevant encumbrances was available in the public domain and the buyer did not avail itself of the opportunity to review the relevant public registers.[54]

[226] Conceptually, Russian law[55] differentiates between two types of warranties:

(1) warranties relating to the shares being sold – in relation to the title to the shares or warranties in relation to the business, in which case, the rules on quality of goods should apply, in addition to the provisions of the Civil Code on warranties,
(2) warranties not directly relating to the shares but still important for the receiving party (e.g., those relating to the financial status of a party, availability of permits and approvals), in which case general rules on damages apply, in addition to the warranties provisions of the Civil Code.

[54] Resolution of the sixteenth appellate court on case No. A63-1976/2017 of 3 October 2017.
[55] Resolution of the Plenum of the Supreme Court of Russian Federation No. 49 of 25 December 2018.

The practical difference between these two approaches is that while the law expressly allows limitation of general contractual damages (in relation to (2) above), it is silent whether the damages in relation to the quality of goods may be limited by contract, so, arguably, the liability for breach of warranties in relation to (1) are regulated by the Civil Code and cannot be altered by contract.

[227] There are a few types of remedies for breach of warranties that are granted by law or may be provided by the parties in the share purchase agreement:

(1) damages in accordance with general rules – the amount of such damages will be determined as the amount required to put the injured party in the position it would have been in had the warranty not been breached;
(2) penalty, if the contract provides for a penalty for breach of warranty. Depending on the agreement of the parties such penalties may be inclusive of any contractual damages or be recovered in addition to such damages. It should be noted that while the law allows the parties to agree penalties for breach of warranty, they are rarely used in practice given complexities in agreeing on the amount of penalties payable for a particular breach;
(3) if the breach of warranty is material, in addition to claiming damages or penalties, the injured party has the right to rescind the contract. Such right of rescission may be excluded by the agreement of the parties;
(4) if the breach of warranty constitutes deceit or a substantive misunderstanding caused by false representation, the injured party also has the right to claim in court that the contract is void. This statutory right cannot be waived by contract.

5.9 Indemnities under Russian Law

[228] Pursuant to Article 406.1, the parties to an agreement (including a corporate agreement or a sale and purchase agreement related to the sale of shares or participatory interests) entered into in the course of their business activities may agree on an obligation to compensate each other for any 'property losses'[56] incurred upon the occurrence of certain events specified in the agreement and not related to the breach of an obligation under such agreement. Examples would include losses caused by the performance of an obligation being impossible to fulfil and losses caused as a result of claims by third parties or state authorities, etc.[57]

[229] An agreement containing an indemnity clause must specify the amount of compensation payable under the indemnity or establish a procedure for its calculation. In principle, the courts must respect such a provision and they are not

[56] The Civil Code does not provide a definition of 'property losses' and as such it is unclear whether (and, if so, to what extent) such 'property losses' correspond with the damages recoverable for breach of agreement defined in Art. 15 of the Civil Code.

[57] Article 406.1(1) of the Civil Code.

entitled to decrease the amount of compensation payable under the indemnity unless it is proven that the indemnified party has deliberately contributed to an increase in the amount of its losses.

[230] The Russian Supreme Court[58] has further clarified that, unlike a claim for damages, compensation of property losses is available under an indemnity irrespective of whether there has been a breach of an obligation by the indemnifying party, and therefore there is no requirement to prove a causal connection between a breach and the losses caused.

[231] Under the literal wording of Article 406.1, an agreement on compensation can only be concluded with respect to the property losses of a party to the agreement itself and not, for instance, such party's affiliates or shareholders. Recovery of compensation for the losses of such third parties may be possible to the extent that such losses represent property losses of a party to the agreement.[59] However, any compensation would in any event be payable only to a party to the agreement, and not to a third party.

5.10 Economic Substance Behind Warranties/ Indemnities

[232] Structures that are used to secure seller's liability (in a situation where the seller does not have material assets) for breach of warranties is not different to those used in other countries and includes:

- suretyship or independent guarantee of the ultimate beneficial owner of the seller;
- holding back the agreed part of consideration – in the purchaser's hands or in a segregated escrow account.

5.11 Independent Guarantee

[233] Independent guarantee is one of the instruments used to secure obligations of a party. Under an independent guarantee, the guarantor undertakes, at the request of a principal, to pay a certain amount to a specified third party (beneficiary) in accordance with the terms of the guarantee and irrespective of the validity of the obligation secured by the guarantee (i.e., the guarantor's obligation to the beneficiary is independent of the principal obligation secured by the guarantee).

[58] Resolution No. 7 'On Application by the Courts of Certain Provisions of the Civil Code Relating to Contractual Liability' dated 24 March 2016.

[59] For example, losses of a subsidiary may indirectly constitute 'property losses' of the parent company if they result in the decrease of the value of the asset (i.e., the subsidiary) owned by such parent company.

In other words, the independent guarantee is an independent obligation, i.e., it does not terminate upon termination of the principal obligation.

[234] The guarantor has the right of recourse against the principal in the amount which has been paid in accordance with the terms of the guarantee (unless an agreement on issuance of the guarantee provides otherwise). The amount of the guarantee can be decreased or increased upon a specified term or event, if so provided by the guarantee. The guarantor can only raise objections to the beneficiary's claims based on the guarantee and not the underlying agreement or undertaking. The independent guarantee can be revoked or amended by the guarantor only if it is provided so in such independent guarantee.

5.12 Suretyship Agreement

[235] Under Russian law,[60] suretyship is a well-tested and widely used instrument to secure obligations. Suretyship can be issued by corporate entities and individuals. Generally, suretyship is used to receive security from individuals (who are not allowed to issue independent guarantees). Unlike an independent guarantee, the suretyship obligation is of an ancillary nature to the principal obligation, i.e., a suretyship obligation terminates upon the termination of the obligation which it secures. The suretyship may secure (among other things): (i) monetary or non-monetary obligations; and (ii) future obligations.

[236] As a general rule, the surety is fully liable for the debtor's non-performance or improper performance of the secured obligation and the surety's liability is joint and several with the debtor's liability, unless the suretyship agreement provides for the secondary liability of the surety or imposes any limits on its liability. If the secured obligation is amended so as to increase the surety's liability without its consent, the surety will remain liable on the previous terms. The surety is entitled to raise against the creditor the same objections as those which could be raised by the debtor. Upon payment to the creditor, the surety has a right of subrogation against the debtor (i.e., steps into the shoes of the creditor).

[237] If the surety does not voluntarily perform its obligations under the suretyship agreement, the creditor can file a claim against the surety in court.

5.13 Limitations of the Seller's Liability

[238] The types of limitations on the seller's liability available under Russian law are similar to those existing in other jurisdictions. Examples of such limitations agreed in the share purchase agreement include:

- a provision that the seller is not liable for losses relating to matters disclosed to the purchaser;

[60] Articles 361–367 of the Civil Code.

- a *de minimis* threshold, under which the seller is not liable for a claim unless the purchaser's losses exceed a certain value;
- a 'basket' provision, under which the seller is not liable for claims by the purchaser unless the aggregate amount of losses for which the seller is otherwise liable exceed a certain threshold;
- monetary caps which limit the seller's total liability to a specific figure; and
- time-based limitations, whereby the seller is not liable if the purchaser filed a claim after the expiry of an agreed period of time.

[239] Russian law expressly allows the parties to agree that upon breach of contract the amounts payable may be less than the actual damages. However, in the case of breach of warranties in relation to the shares or target's business, the position of the Supreme Court should be noted that the damages for breach of such warranties should be payable in accordance with the rules for breach of requirements to the quality of goods. The law is silent whether liability for the quality of goods may be limited by contract – the Supreme Commercial Court clarified[61] that the law does not preclude the parties to agree on the consequences of breach of quality requirements other than those provided in the Civil Code, but still left open the question whether the liability can be waived or reduced by contract.

[240] With regard to time-based limitations, the general statute of limitations for breach of contract is three years, beginning from the moment when a party discovered (or should have discovered) the breach. Russian law expressly provides that any agreement of the parties altering the statute of limitations is void,[62] and thus the parties to an agreement cannot provide for time-related limitations different from the statutory periods.

[241] However, there is an alternative position under Russian law, whereby the provisions of an agreement related to the deadline for bringing claims is not an agreement to change the statutory period specified in Article 198 of the Civil Code, but rather a deadline for bringing claims in connection with defective goods under Article 477 of the Civil Code. In accordance with Article 477, the parties can agree on a warranty period with respect to sold goods (or shares), and the purchaser is entitled to bring claims relating to defects in the goods within such period of time. Another alternative used in practice is the agreement of the parties that the amount of losses payable for breach of warranties is substantially reduced if the claim is made upon expiry of the agreed period of time.

5.14 Post-closing Obligations of the Parties

[242] It is sometimes commercially agreed that for a certain period of time (e.g., three years) following completion, the seller in an M&A transaction will undertake to refrain from competing with the target company's business, soliciting the target

[61] Resolution of the Plenum of the Supreme Court of Russian Federation No. 16 of 14 March 2014, para. 4.

[62] Article 198 of the Civil Code.

company's employees or soliciting the target company's clients, suppliers or customers. The enforceability of such non-compete obligations in Russia is controversial.

5.15 Non-compete Obligation

[243] The Russian Law on Protection of Competition[63] (the 'Russian Competition Law') does not contain any specific provisions in relation to non-compete provisions in sale and purchase agreements or shareholders' agreements. Such non-compete provisions are therefore regulated by the general provisions of the Russian Competition Law. Under Article 11(1) of the Russian Competition Law, any agreements between competitors which may lead to the territorial division of the relevant market are prohibited. Such agreements are considered to constitute 'cartels' and are illegal per se, in the sense that their anti-competitive effect on the market is presumed and does not have to be established and proved by the Russian FAS.

[244] The Russian Competition Law[64] also prohibits any other agreements between entities (whether or not competitors) if the FAS establishes and proves that such agreements result or may result in the restriction of competition on a particular market.[65]

[245] There are only a very limited number of exceptions to these restrictions that are expressly set out in the Russian Competition Law. In particular, under Article 13 of the Russian Competition Law, non-compete restrictions in joint venture agreements that violate Article 11(1) may be considered permissible if, as a result of entering into such agreements: (i) competition in the market is not eliminated; (ii) restrictions are not imposed on third parties; and (iii) certain positive effects are achieved (e.g., consumers would benefit from the arrangement, technical progress will be enhanced). In practice, in the absence of guidelines from the FAS, it may be very difficult to establish that an agreement satisfies these criteria.

[246] The FAS generally takes a negative position with respect to non-compete clauses in sale and purchase agreements, even when the agreement is between non-competing entities. For the most part, the FAS views such clauses as leading (or

[63] Federal Law No. 135-FZ 'On the Protection of Competition' dated 26 July 2006.

[64] Article 11(4) of the Law on Protection of Competition.

[65] Article 4(17) of the Russian Competition Law provides that a limitation of competition on the market may be indicated by: a decline in the number of entities other than members of the same group on the market; an increase or decrease in the price of goods that is unrelated to any changes to other general conditions governing the circulation of such goods on the market; the renunciation by entities other than members of the same group of independent actors on a given market of goods; determination of the general conditions governing the circulation of goods on the relevant market by an agreement between companies, or in accordance with instructions issued by another person that are binding on them, or as a result of entities other than members of the same group coordinating their actions on a particular market of goods; and other circumstances allowing an entity or several entities unilaterally to influence the general conditions of turnover of goods on the market.

potentially leading) to: (i) the division of a market by territory or by the composition of buyers or customers; and/or (ii) the creation of barriers to the entry of new participants (i.e., a seller and its affiliates) onto the market. Thus, it may be the case that the relevant non-compete provisions will be deemed unenforceable in Russia. Currently, the only way to be sure that non-compete obligations in an agreement are enforceable is to submit an agreement that raises potential competition law concerns to the FAS in order to seek its approval that the agreement complies with the Russian Completion Law and is enforceable in Russia.

[247] If the FAS discovers the existence of non-compete undertakings which have not been previously cleared with it and concludes that they are not in line with the Russian Competition Law, it may decide to impose fines based on the turnover of the parties to such arrangement. The statutory amount of such fines ranges from 1% to 15% of a party's turnover from the distribution of goods or services in the market where the violation occurred (mostly likely the Russian market only), but not less than RUB100 000 (approximately USD1 500).[66]

5.16 Non-solicitation Obligation

[248] Russian employment law[67] does not include any regulations with respect to non-solicitation undertakings (i.e., an undertaking not to approach employees with the aim of persuading them to change employment) as such.

[249] Although the Civil Code recognizes negative obligations (i.e., obligations to refrain from certain actions),[68] the Civil Code does not permit the limitation of the legal capacity of an individual or a legal entity by agreement unless such limitation is expressly prescribed for by law.[69] Furthermore, the Civil Code provides that the waiver of civil law rights by individuals and legal entities does not terminate those rights, unless otherwise provided by law.[70] Thus, it may be argued that a contractual obligation to refrain from taking certain actions in cases that are not expressly provided by Russian law is not enforceable.

[250] Furthermore, under Russian employment law, an employer may not refuse to enter into an employment agreement with a candidate whose skills and qualifications meet the requirements established by the employer or by law for a specific position.[71] Since non-solicitation undertakings also imply an obligation, among others, not to hire certain candidates for reasons not relevant to their professional qualification, such an undertaking may be viewed as contradicting Russian employment law, or even as discriminatory, and therefore may be held to be unenforceable. Refusal to employ gives the prospective employee the right to challenge such

[66] However, the risk of fines actually being imposed is only theoretical.

[67] The Labor Code of the Russian Federation No. 197-FZ dated 30 December 2001 (the *'Labor Code'*).

[68] Article 307 of the Civil Code.

[69] Articles 22 and 49 of the Civil Code.

[70] Article 9 of the Civil Code.

[71] Article 64 of the Labor Code.

refusal (if he is otherwise qualified for the job) and also such refusal may be subject to an administrative fine of up to RUB50 000.[72]

[251] Should a court confirm the validity of a non-solicitation undertaking, arguably damages may be claimed for failure to comply with it. However, the party claiming damages must prove the amount of its loss. Should the agreement provide for a penalty for breach of the non-solicitation obligation, the non-breaching party is not obliged to prove its actual losses. Courts may, however, reduce the penalty to a reasonable amount if the penalty substantially exceeds the damage inflicted.[73] Courts often exercise their authority to reduce penalties in this way.

5.17 Break Fee

[252] A break fee arrangement may be agreed whereby one of the parties (most commonly the seller) wishes to achieve a high degree of deal certainty. The Civil Code expressly allows parties to include in their agreement a specific fee (break fee) payable in the event of unilateral termination of the agreement by a party.[74]

5.18 Option Agreements

[253] Russian law provides for two types of option agreements have been introduced into the Civil Code:

(1) an option to conclude an agreement;[75] and
(2) an option agreement.[76]

---

72 Article 5.27 of the 'Code of Administrative Offences of the Russian Federation' No. 195-FZ dated 30 December 2001.

73 Article 333 of the Civil Code.

74 Article 310(3) of the Civil Code.

75 Article 429.2 of the Civil Code. Under an option to conclude an agreement, one party, in return for a fee or other consideration, makes an irrevocable offer to the other party to conclude one or several agreements by accepting the offer. Art. 429.2 further provides that the option must specify the subject of the agreement to be concluded by exercising the option in a way that allows it to be identified at the time of acceptance, as well all other essential terms of the agreement. Art. 429.2 expressly provides that the option to conclude an agreement may specify that acceptance is possible only upon the occurrence of a specific condition, which may include a condition whose fulfilment depends on one party's will.

76 Article 429.3 of the Civil Code. Pursuant to the provisions of Art. 429.3 of the Civil Code, the parties to an existing agreement may agree that one party will undertake to perform certain actions (including paying a sum of money, transferring or receiving property) as specified in the agreement upon the request of the other party, while the other party undertakes to pay a certain fee as payment for the right to request that performance. If the other party fails to request the performance within the specified period of time, the option agreement is terminated. The option agreement may provide that the performance request is deemed to be made if certain circumstances specified in the agreement occur.

[254] The main difference between these two types of agreements is that under an option to conclude an agreement a party acquires the right to conclude, in the future, one or more separate agreements (e.g., a sale and purchase agreement) with the other party.

[255] By contrast, under an option agreement the party acquires the right to require the other party to perform certain actions (e.g., to transfer shares). In other words, unlike an option to conclude an agreement, the option agreement itself constitutes an agreement allowing the exercise of the option (e.g., a sale and purchase of shares).

[256] Transaction with participatory interest in LLCs requires certification of a notary – the following mechanism is provided by the LLC Law:[77]

- The seller issues an irrevocable offer, which is subject to notarial certification (if the irrevocable offer is included in the option agreement, such option agreement itself should be certified by a notary).
- After the acceptance of the irrevocable offer (or occurrence of the conditions specified in the option agreement[78]), the acceptance also needs to be certified by a notary (upon such certification, the irrevocable offer is deemed to have been accepted by the purchaser). Notification of acceptance of the offer by the purchaser is then sent to the seller.
- The notary must, within two business days, submit an application to the registration authority in order to reflect the transfer of the ownership rights to the participatory interests in the USRLE.

6 SPECIFIC RULES ON PUBLIC TAKEOVERS

6.1 Legislative Background

[257] There are potentially a few situations that may arise in the context of mergers and acquisitions in relation to public companies:

- VTO if the offer is made to all shareholders in the target company;
- MTO if more than 30% of the shares are acquired; and
- squeeze-out if the purchaser consolidated more than 95% of the shares in the target company and wished to expel the remaining shareholders.

[77] Federal Law No. 391-FZ 'On Amendments to Certain Legislative Acts of the Russian Federation' dated 29 December 2015 (the amendments came into force on 15 January 2016).

[78] Pursuant to Art. 21(11) of the LLC Law, if an irrevocable offer has been made conditional on the occurrence of conditions precedent or conditions subsequent, the party accepting an offer must provide the notary with evidence on the occurrence or non-occurrence of the relevant condition.

[258] There are two main ways to acquire a significant stake (i.e., more than 30%) in a public joint stock company: (i) the purchaser can approach individual shareholders to buy their shares; and (ii) the purchaser can make a public offer to all shareholders in accordance with the VTO or MTO procedures, as discussed below.

6.2 Voluntary Tender Offer

[259] In order to acquire more than 30% of voting shares of a public joint stock company,[79] a prospective purchaser can submit a VTO to the company. A VTO is a public offer addressed to all owners of the voting shares of the company (such offer can also be made to the owners of securities convertible into ordinary shares) to acquire their shares. The purchaser under a VTO can determine the purchase price of securities and the size of the stake it intends to purchase at its own discretion.

[260] VTOs can be conditional on the number of shares that the purchaser intends to acquire, i.e., the offer can be deemed expired if the purchaser failed to accumulate the target percentage of shares.

[261] After submission of a VTO, it cannot be revoked by the purchaser until expiration of the relevant acceptance period unless the offer provides otherwise. During the acceptance period, the purchaser is prohibited from acquiring the company's shares/securities on any terms and conditions other than those set out in the submitted VTO.

[262] Together with the VTO, the purchaser must secure a bank guarantee sufficient to purchase up to 100% of the shares in the target company. The law sets forth detailed regulations on the tender offer submission procedure (further discussed below) and establishes restrictions on the target company, as well as additional disclosure obligations applicable once a respective tender offer is submitted.

[263] If a VTO complies with MTO requirements, then the purchaser does not have to make an MTO upon reaching the threshold of 30%, 50% or 75% of voting shares. MTOs are further discussed below.

6.3 Mandatory Tender Offer

[264] An MTO must be made within thirty-five days following the date when a person (on his own or together with affiliates) acquired more than 30%, 50% or 75% of the voting shares in a public company or securities convertible into such shares on the basis of a negotiated transaction or a VTO not compliant with the MTO requirements. The MTO requirements also apply in a situation where unaffiliated entities become affiliated and hold together more than 30% of voting shares.

[79] The law does not regulate acquisition of less than 30% of shares in public companies.

[265] There are a number of exemptions from the requirement to make an MTO, including:

- establishment or reorganization of a company;
- transfer of shares between affiliates;
- buyback of the shares by the company;
- acquisition of shares by the shareholder on the basis of the pre-emptive right to acquire newly issued shares of a company; or
- acquisition of shares as a result of a VTO which satisfies all requirements applicable to an MTO.

6.4 Failure to Make MTO

[266] If the purchaser of more than 30% stake in a public company fails to make a MTO:

- The shares owned by such purchaser and its affiliates in excess of the 30%, 50% or 75% threshold lose the attached voting rights until a proper MTO is launched; for example, if the purchaser acquired 55% of the shares, he will be able to vote only 30% of shares. This voting limitation does not affect the purchaser's right to receive dividends.
- In addition, the purchaser may be subject to an administrative fine in the amount of up to RUB500 000 (approximately USD8 000).
- Potentially, compensation of losses of the minority shareholders – although this remedy is not expressly provided by law, there was one case[80] where minority shareholders successfully claimed losses in a situation where the purchaser failed to make a MTO.

[267] Shareholders cannot demand specific performance in relation to the purchaser's obligation to make an MTO.

6.5 MTO: Price

[268] The price under an MTO should be not less than:

- If the company is traded on a stock exchange – the highest of (i) the price at which the purchaser acquired the shares (in a private transaction or non-compliant VTO) during six months prior to the date of submission of the MTO, (ii) the price which the purchaser promised to pay for the shares in the company six months prior to the date of submission of the MTO and (iii) the weighted average stock exchange price for the six-month period preceding the submission of the MTO.

[80] Case in relation to Stroyexpo No. 40-121504/12 of 8 July 2016.

- If the company is not traded on a stock exchange – the highest of (i) and (ii) above and the market price of shares determined by the valuation of an independent appraiser.

6.6 Tender Offer Submission

[269] The tender offer (either MTO or VTO) must be accompanied by a bank guarantee securing potential payment obligations of the purchaser, which must meet, *inter alia*, the following requirements:

- the amount of the guarantee should be equal to the aggregate purchase price of all shares that potentially may be acquired under the offer, i.e., up to 100% of the shares of the company;
- the bank guarantee should be irrevocable;
- the bank guarantee may not require the beneficiaries of the guarantee (i.e., the selling shareholders) to provide documents that are not envisaged by law; and
- the term of the bank guarantee should be sufficient to cover the duration of the tender offer procedure plus six months after the proposed purchase price payment date set forth in the tender offer.

[270] Bank guarantees are generally considered an onerous obligation since the amount cannot be reduced, even in a situation where the prospective sellers waive the MTO in advance or during the MTO procedure.

[271] If the target is not a listed company, the purchaser under the MTO also needs to arrange for the preparation of an independent appraiser's report in order to determine the purchase price of the securities expected to be acquired.

[272] Submission of the tender offer generally includes the following steps:

- filing a tender offer with the Central Bank at least fifteen days prior to its submission to the target;
- submission of the tender offer along with accompanying documents to the target for further communication to its shareholders;
- upon receipt of the tender offer, the board of directors adopts recommendations in relation to the tender offer which include, *inter alia*, assessment of the proposed purchase price and the plans of the potential purchaser in relation to the target and its employees;
- communicating the tender offer and the recommendations of the board of directors to the shareholders no later than fifteen days after the receipt of the tender offer by the target. The recommendation must also be communicated to the potential purchaser who initiated the tender offer;
- filing a report on the results of the tender offer with the Central Bank and the target no later than thirty days following the deadline for acceptance of the tender offer.

[273] The owners of the shares can accept the received tender offer by submitting 'acceptance applications' to the registrar of the target company. All acceptance applications submitted to the registrar are deemed submitted to the potential purchaser. The time limits for acceptance of a tender offer once it is received by the target company must be set out in the tender offer and may vary:

- Under the MTO procedure – from 70 up to 80 days; and
- Under the VTO procedure – from 70 up to 90 days.

6.7 Limitations on the Target after the Tender Offer Is Submitted

[274] After the tender offer's submission to the target company and until the expiry of twenty days (or, in certain cases, a longer period) following the deadline for the tender offer acceptance, the board of directors and the executive bodies of the target company must not, without the approval of the general shareholders' meeting, make any decisions or take actions which may result, *inter alia*, in:

- the target company entering into any interested party transactions;
- the target company entering into transactions exceeding 10% of the book value of the company's assets (unless made in the ordinary course of business); and
- the target company issuing shares and convertible securities.

[275] Transactions entered into by the target company in violation of the aforementioned limitations can be invalidated by a court at the request of a shareholder of the target company, the company itself or by the purchaser who initiated the tender offer.

6.8 Squeeze-Out

[276] A shareholder that acquires, as a result of a tender offer (an MTO or VTO made to all shareholders of a public joint stock company), more than 95% of the voting shares of the target company (the '*Majority Shareholder*') may require the remaining shareholders to sell their shares (a so-called squeeze-out) provided that the Majority Shareholder acquired not less than 10% of the voting shares under the tender offer.

[277] The JSC Law stipulates that the price for squeezed-out shares should not be less than:

(a) their market value as determined by an independent appraiser;
(b) the price indicated in the tender offer as a result of which the Majority Shareholder exceeded the 95% threshold; and
(c) the highest price for which the Majority Shareholder (or its affiliates) acquired (or agreed to acquire) the target shares from third parties after expiration of the time period for acceptance of the tender offer referred to in (b) above.

6.9 Main Steps of the Squeeze-Out Procedure/ Documents

[278] In order to exercise its squeeze-out right, the Majority Shareholder has to:

- obtain a conclusion of an independent appraiser on the market price of the voting shares which are subject to the buyout;
- file with the Central Bank a written buyout demand containing detailed information on the terms of the proposed buyout including the offered purchase price; and
- deliver the buyout demand to the target company upon the expiration of fifteen days following its filing with the Central Bank (with any amendments required by the Central Bank in order to bring the buyout demand into compliance with the statutory requirements).

[279] The Majority Shareholder must submit the buyout demand to the target company within six months from the deadline for the shareholders to accept the tender offer preceding the squeeze-out.

6.10 State Control over Acquisition of Shares in Public JSCs

[280] The Central Bank exercises control over the acquisition of significant stakes in public joint stock companies and squeeze-out procedures. An MTO, VTO or buyout demand must be first submitted to the Central Bank for its review before submission of the relevant document to the target company. The purchaser must also provide the Central Bank with notarized copies of the documents which should accompany the MTO, VTO or buyout demand when it is submitted to the company.

[281] The Central Bank generally has fifteen days to review the submitted documents, and if it finds that the documents do not comply with the statutory requirements, it may demand that the purchaser eliminate revealed violations and resubmit the revised documents for inspection. If the Central Bank does not issue its ruling within the fifteen-day review period, it can still initiate court proceedings in order to cause the purchaser to bring the documents into compliance with the statutory requirements.

[282] Fifteen calendar days after the date of submission of the documents to the Central Bank, the purchaser may submit the MTO, VTO or buyout demand to the target company, as long as there are no comments from the Central Bank.

7 FINANCING OPTIONS FOR ACQUISITIONS

[283] Financing of a business acquisition in Russia can be done using a variety of structures, depending on the commercial considerations, size of the project and proposed financing parties.

[284] When a loan (whether by a Russian or a foreign lender) is provided to and repaid by the buyer, and is secured by the buyer's assets, the structure is relatively straightforward. In such case, the lender primarily relies on the buyer's balance sheet and the security provided by it.

[285] Implementing a more 'classic' leveraged buyout structure in Russia, in which the loan is repaid by the acquired target, requires taking into account a number of specific considerations which are described below:

Illustrative Example of Implementing a Leveraged Buyout Structure in Russia

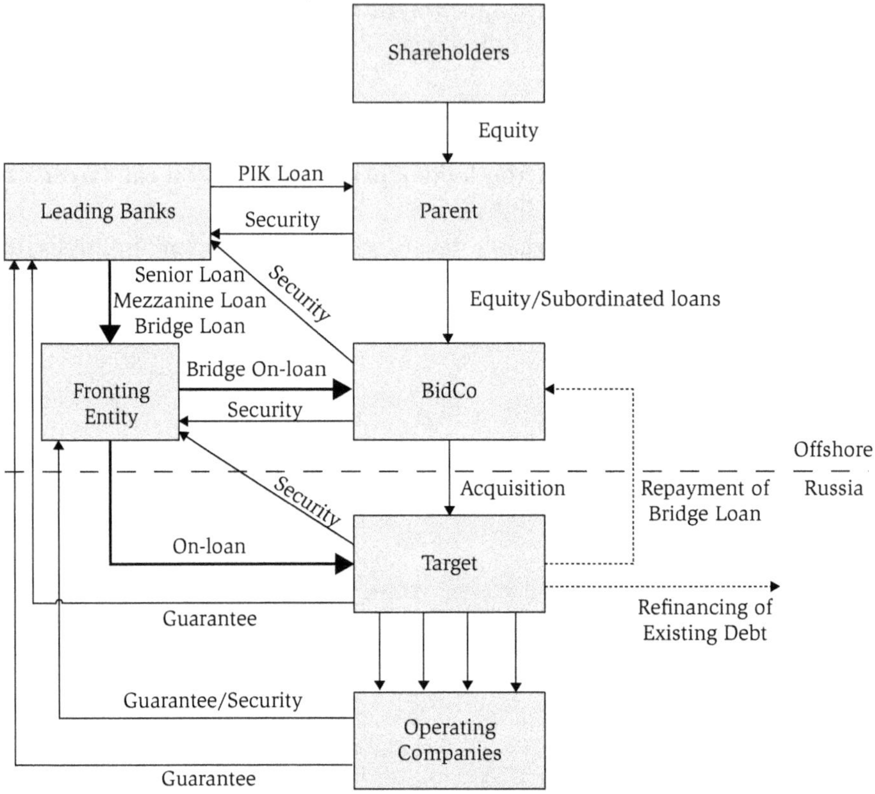

7.1 Security for Loans: Prior to Acquisition

[286] The financers of a leveraged buyout (LBO) project ideally prefer to have a pledge of the purchased shares in the target company as a condition precedent to the disbursement of the loan. However, in the absence of financing, the buyer is not always able to actually acquire such shares, and the seller is often unwilling to pledge them to the buyer's prospective lenders.

[287] This interdependence has to be addressed in each individual case. By way of example, the diagram illustrates the structure where the lenders first provide a bridge loan to the buyer, which can be used by the buyer (together with a certain amount of its own funds) to acquire and become the registered owner of the shares in the target company. As soon as this is complete, the second, often larger portion of the loan is provided by the lenders (in Russia often to the target itself), such loan is secured by a pledge of the newly acquired shares. This second loan is used to procure repayment of the bridge and also to fund other acquisition-related needs.

[288] Sponsors (companies controlling the entity that acquires the target) may be required to provide additional coverage and support for the loans in the interim period until the acquisition is actually completed.

7.2 Security for Loans: Upon Completion of Acquisition

[289] Security packages typically include a combination of foreign and Russian law security.

[290] The foreign security is normally a standard set of share pledges over certain non-Russian entities, fixed and floating charges over assets, guarantees, bank account charges and assignments of inter-company subordinated loans (if any).

[291] A Russian security package can include pledges and mortgages over material assets, share pledges over Russian companies of the target group, pledges of goods in circulation (inventories), and pledges of contract rights.

[292] Particular attention should be paid to structuring the Russian security package for a multi-lender (e.g., syndicated or club) loan. Although Russian law provides for the possibility to create security in favour of multiple creditors and allows appointing a pledge manager who would act in the interests of the lenders, special structuring is still needed in international financing deals.

[293] Structures that are can be considered in secured financings with multiple lenders are as follows:

(i) A 'joint and several structure', whereby Russian security is granted to secure the borrower's payment obligations to one of the lenders who is a joint and several creditor with the other lenders for the payment obligations of the borrower.
(ii) A 'fronting entity structure', whereby Russian security is granted to secure the borrower's payment obligations to a fronting entity which receives financing from the lenders and then lends the loan proceeds to the borrower. The lenders would benefit from the Russian law security indirectly by having robust security over the shares and assets of the fronting entity.
(iii) Consecutively ranked pledge agreements, whereby consecutively ranked Russian security interests are granted to each secured lender, with the secured lenders' *pari passu* ranking restored in an offshore security sharing agreement. It may be impractical where there are a large number of secured lenders.
(iv) A single unranked instrument (co-pledge holders), whereby Russian security is granted to the secured lenders in a single instrument (pledge agreement) to which all secured lenders are parties. This may be impractical where loan transfers are anticipated, as each loan transfer would require updating the relevant pledge registers to reflect the up-to-date composition of the syndicate.

(v) Appointment of a pledge manager who would act in the name of and in the interests of secured lenders. However, it is the lenders (rather than the pledge manager) who must be registered as pledge holders in the relevant pledge registers relating to participation interest pledges and mortgages, which makes the structure impractical where those types of pledges are used and loan transfers are anticipated (for the same reason as described in item (iv) above). Furthermore, using this structure for foreign law syndicates would not be free from legal uncertainties.

[294] A 'parallel debt structure', whereby Russian security is granted to a 'security beneficiary' to secure the borrower's covenant to pay that security beneficiary an amount which equals its payment obligations to the lenders in respect of the senior loans.

7.3 Debt Pushdown

[295] One of the key requirements for an LBO structure is to ensure that debt provided for the purposes of acquisition is serviced by the acquired target. Classic techniques, e.g., merger debt pushdown or repayment of debt by an entity that did not originally receive the loan, are not practically achievable when the target is a Russian legal entity. One possible option, as mentioned above, is to structure the financing as a two-stage process. First, a bridge loan is provided to the buyer's bid company to allow completion of the acquisition. Second, the main portion of the loan is provided to the target (and partially used to repay the bridge loan). As a result, the target will act as the borrower under the acquisition loan.

7.4 Subordination Issues

[296] LBO financing usually involves different groups of creditors (e.g., senior, mezzanine, payment-in-kind lenders and others), whose claims against the borrower are subordinated, respectively. With limited exceptions, the Russian Bankruptcy Law[81] does not expressly allow the contractual subordination of claims of different creditors. Therefore, in addition to intercreditor deeds, it is not uncommon for lenders in Russian transactions to consider structural subordination. Lenders providing loans to the level closer to the operating assets are typically deemed to be in a senior position compared to those lenders who have provided loans at the holding company level. Certain other structuring techniques can also be used to achieve subordination to the maximum possible extent.

[81] Federal Law No. 127-FZ 'On Insolvency (Bankruptcy)' dated 26 October 2002.

7.5 Regulatory Aspects

[297] As discussed above in more detail, acquisition deals may be subject to certain consent or filing requirements under Russian laws on foreign investments (including in strategic sectors) and antimonopoly control. The same considerations would be relevant to the acquisition of Russian assets under the enforcement of the relevant security instruments.

[298] Project cash flows should be carefully structured in accordance with Russian currency control regulations. Although many earlier restrictions have been removed, certain limitations and filing requirements remain. This relates primarily to the currency repatriation requirement (i.e., the obligation of Russian residents to receive funds due from foreign counterparties: (i) for exported goods and services, (ii) for goods and services that had been paid but were not imported, or (iii) under loan agreements, in residents' accounts in Russia); registration requirement with respect to loan agreements and foreign trade contracts, and a special regime of offshore bank accounts of Russian residents.

[299] The financial assistance available to parties of a transaction that are incorporated in various jurisdictions should also be taken into account. For a Russian company to enter into a transaction with (or for the benefit of) its affiliate, specific corporate authorizations may be required. Such authorization has to be approved by disinterested (independent) board members or shareholders, depending on the size of the transaction.

7.6 Acquisition of Less than 100% in the Target

[300] Structuring an LBO for the acquisition of less than 100% of the shares in the target company can be substantially more complicated, and implementing the transaction can take additional time.

[301] This is because such transactions usually require the provision of security and sureties by the target and its subsidiaries. If any minority shareholders remain in the target following the acquisition, most likely such shareholders will have the decisive vote on the target's entry into the majority of transaction documents (because the buyer of the shares in the target will likely be qualified as an 'interested person' for corporate approval procedures of such transactions). Consequently, full cooperation between the buyer and other shareholders of the target company will be necessary to allow for smooth implementation of the transaction.

[302] In addition, the acquisition of less than 100% of the shares may trigger the application of mandatory buyout or offer procedures envisaged by Russian corporate law.

7.7 Control over the Transfer of Funds

[303] In cross-border transactions, both residents and non-residents are subject to currency regulations. The key legislation in this area is the Law on Currency Control[82] and a number of subordinate acts issued by the currency regulatory bodies, i.e., the Central Bank and the Russian Government.

[304] Currency regulations in Russia have been significantly liberalized over the past years. The general rule is that all currency operations with respect to which no restrictions have been imposed or special regulation introduced may be performed freely. Moreover, currency operations do not require any individual permits from any state bodies.

7.8 Operations Between Residents and Non-residents

[305] Currency control restrictions often apply differently to residents and non-residents.

[306] For currency control purposes, (i) Russian companies (as well as their branches and any other departments located outside Russia), (ii) Russian citizens, and (iii) foreign citizens or apatrides who are permanently resident in Russia based on a residence permit under the Russian law are regarded as residents.

[307] Foreign companies established under foreign law outside of Russia (as well as their branches located inside Russia) and foreign citizens or apatrides who are not residents for currency control purposes are regarded as non-residents.

[308] The general rule established by the Law on Currency Control is that all currency operations between residents and non-residents (e.g., repayment of foreign loans, payment of fees and charges to foreign companies for IP or technology) may be freely conducted unless they are specifically restricted by law.[83]

[309] As of 1 March 2018, residents are required to register certain agreements concluded with non-residents with authorized Russian banks (this procedure replaces the previous filing requirement known as 'opening of the transaction passport' and is intended to be easier than filing a transaction passport). These include agreements underlying, *inter alia*: (i) loans; (ii) the import or export of goods, services and IP (including agency, commission and similar agreements), and (iii) leasing and financial leasing of movables and immovables.[84]

---

[82] Federal Law No. 173-FZ 'On Currency Regulation and Currency Control' dated 10 December 2003.

[83] The rule for currency operations between residents is the opposite: they are generally prohibited.

[84] Instruction No. 181-I of the Central Bank 'On the Procedure for the Presentation by Residents and Non-Residents to Authorized Banks of Confirming Documents and Information for Carrying Out Currency Operations [. . .]', dated 16 August 2017.

[310] Currency control is carried out by the authorized currency control bodies, including the Central Bank, the Federal Tax Service and the Federal Customs Service, and currency control agents, including authorized Russian banks and professional participants in the securities market. The Central Bank exercises control over financial organizations, the Federal Customs Service over currency operations related to the export and import of goods from/to Russia and the Federal Tax Service over residents' and non-residents' compliance with the currency legislation in other areas. While both currency control agents and currency control bodies monitor compliance with the currency regulations, the latter are also entitled to impose sanctions for their violation.

7.9 Off-Shore Bank Accounts of Russian Residents

[311] In general, Russian residents (except for some categories, such as, for example, certain state officials) may open and maintain foreign bank accounts, although notification procedures apply.

[312] Russian residents are required to notify the tax authorities at their place of registration of the opening (and closing) of any such account not later than one month from the date of opening (or closing) the relevant account.[85] In addition, Russian residents are required to provide the tax authorities at their place of registration in Russia with reports showing the movement of funds to and from such accounts.[86]

[313] The use of residents' accounts abroad is subject to certain restrictions set out in the Law on Currency Control. Thus, the list of cases when funds may be credited to residents' accounts abroad is limited to cases specifically provided by the Law on Currency Control. Such cases include, *inter alia*: (i) the transfer of funds by residents from their other bank accounts in Russia or abroad; (ii) crediting loans from certain lenders to residents' accounts opened in OECD or Financial Action Task Force (FATF) member states (these include foreign currency loans where the lender is a resident of an OECD or FATF member country and the loan is for a term of more than two years, or the lender is an agent of a foreign government). The list of cases when funds may be credited to residents' accounts abroad does not include, for example, the receipt by resident companies of dividends from non-residents or the purchase price for shares sold to a non-resident.[87]

Notably, the opportunities for debiting funds from residents' accounts abroad are much greater than those for crediting funds. Residents may use funds in such accounts to perform any currency operations, save for operations with other residents (though some of them are permitted).

[85] Law on Currency Control, Art. 12(1) and (2).

[86] Law on Currency Control, Art. 12(7).

[87] Law on Currency Control, Art. 12(4, 5, 5.1).

The notification and reporting requirements and restrictions for the use of off-shore accounts do not apply to resident individuals who spend a total of more than 183 days per year abroad.

8 MERGER CONTROLS: ANTITRUST/ COMPETITION ISSUES

8.1 General Regulatory

[314] Most M&A transactions are subject to Russian merger control, which is exercised by the FAS. Prior written consent from the FAS is mandatory if the transaction falls under a category of specific transactions prescribed by law (and subject to specific monetary thresholds also being met). The consent must be obtained before closing the transaction.

[315] Russian merger control procedures are regulated by Federal Law No. 135-FZ 'On the Protection of Competition' which entered into force on 26 October 2006 (the '*Competition Law*'). Since its enactment, the Competition Law has been amended several times significantly. The most recent significant amendments entered into force on 5 January 2016.

[316] Current merger control rules cover the following main types of M&A transactions: (i) acquisitions of shares, assets or rights to determine business activities of commercial companies or financial institutions, (ii) mergers and accessions of/between commercial companies and financial institutions, (iii) the establishment of new companies whose charter capital is paid in kind, and (iv) the execution of joint venture agreements between competitors relating to the territory of the Russian Federation.

[317] The Competition Law requires prior FAS consent if as a result of a transaction involving share transfers the purchaser will obtain a right to more than 25%, 50% or 75% of the voting shares in a Russian JSC (or more than 33%, 50% and 66% of participatory shares in a Russian LLC) and provided that the relevant monetary thresholds are met.

[318] If a transaction relates to the shares of a non-Russian company, the application of the regulations will depend on whether the non-Russian target company has Russian subsidiaries or generates sales in Russia.

[319] If a non-Russian target has a Russian subsidiary, the transaction will require prior FAS consent (subject to the relevant monetary thresholds being met) if following completion of the transaction, the purchaser obtains rights to determine the business activities of (or, in other words, 'positive' or 'negative' control over) such Russian subsidiary.

[320] If a non-Russian target does not have a Russian subsidiary, but has generated sales in Russia in excess of RUB1 bn (individually or in aggregate with its group) during the year preceding the year in which the transaction is completed, then acquisitions of more than 50% of the voting shares of such non-Russian company or of rights to determine its business activities will also require prior FAS consent, again subject to relevant monetary thresholds being met.

[321] The monetary thresholds triggering the requirement for prior FAS consent to transactions involving the acquisition of Russian or foreign target companies (except for financial institutions) are as follows: (i) the aggregate worldwide book value of assets of the purchaser, the target, and their groups according to the latest balance sheet exceeding RUB7 bn (approx. EUR100 m) or (ii) the aggregate sales revenues of these entities in the previous calendar year exceeding RUB10 bn (approx. EUR143 m), provided that in cases (i) and (ii) the aggregate worldwide book value of assets of the target company and its group exceed RUB400 m (approx. EUR5.7 m). Calculations of the aggregate assets of the target's group for the purposes of applying the above thresholds do not include the assets of the seller and the seller's group if, as a result of the planned transaction, the seller and its group lose their rights to determine the business activities of the target. Monetary thresholds for financial institutions triggering the obligation to obtain prior FAS consent are set out in separate regulations of the Russian Government. Certain intra-group transactions (such as transactions between parent companies and their direct and indirect subsidiaries and transactions between 'sister companies' owned by the same parent company through a majority stake at all levels of control) are exempt from the requirement to obtain prior FAS consent.

[322] Together with the application, the purchaser (or its representative) submits the documents underlying the transaction (e.g., share purchase agreement, shareholders' agreement), constituent documents of the purchaser and the target and certain other information in relation to the purchaser's and target's groups. Pursuant to the recent amendments to the Competition Law, the FAS must publish information on its official website (www.fas.gov.ru) regarding all applications submitted for its consent and any interested parties may provide the FAS with information or their opinion on the influence of the transaction on competition.

[323] Under the Competition Law the purchaser has the right to inform the FAS about the planned transaction before filing an application for consent. The purchaser may submit documents and other supporting information as well as suggest certain conditions for approval of the transaction. The FAS must consider all information and any suggestions in the course of its review of a submitted application.

[324] In the course of reviewing an application, the FAS independently performs a market analysis and assesses the impact of the transaction on competition on the relevant market in Russia. The statutory period for the application review is thirty calendar days following the date when the application was submitted. If the transaction raises competition concerns, the FAS may extend the review period for an additional two months. During the review period, the purchaser may contact the FAS official responsible for the application review to check the status of the review and to address questions if the FAS official has any. Generally, the FAS works quite efficiently in the course of review and cooperates with applicants. The above timing applies equally to all types of transactions. There is no official expedited procedure for review. In practice, the FAS may issue a decision quite quickly if the planned transaction obviously has no impact on competition on the market, or if the FAS has a light workload. This is of course strictly at the FAS' discretion.

[325] If in the course of its review the FAS discovers that the purchaser is a foreign private company or a foreign company controlled by foreign state and/or plans to acquire a Russian entity which performs any of the activities which are considered to be of 'strategic importance' to Russian national defence and security, the FAS extends the review period under the Competition Law until the transaction is cleared under the law on foreign investments. The FAS will dismiss an application under the Competition Law if an application under that law is dismissed.

[326] Following the review of an application, the FAS may: (i) grant an application, (ii) reject an application, or (iii) grant an application together with an order. The Competition Law contains an exhaustive list of cases when the FAS can reject an application (e.g., negative impact on competition on the market as a result of the creation or strengthening of a dominant position of any of the entities involved or failure to provide the FAS with documents or information which is crucial for its assessment of the transaction's impact on competition on the market). In practice, applications are rarely rejected. In most cases where a transaction raises competition concerns, the FAS tends to issue orders on the purchaser rather than reject the application.

[327] There might also be situations when the FAS may issue so-called preliminary/structural conditions to the participants of the transaction. Such conditions must be fulfilled within the term established by the FAS, which may not exceed nine months. The list of the preliminary conditions provided in the Competition Law is open, and includes: setting the procedure for access to manufacturing capacity, infrastructure and information and requirements for the group of any participant of the transaction; requesting a party to dispose of certain assets to third parties unrelated to the purchaser's and the target's groups, etc. Following the submission of documents proving that the conditions have been fulfilled, the FAS must issue its consent to the transaction within thirty days.

[328] The preliminary conditions should be differentiated from the order which is issued together with the approval. The order must be fulfilled only after the parties perform the transaction. The FAS may issue orders, *inter alia,* prohibiting actions which may prevent competition, orders on the execution, termination or amendment of contracts, orders on actions aimed at securing competition, etc.

[329] Failure to obtain prior FAS consent to a transaction may lead to the following negative consequences: (i) imposition of a fine on the purchaser in the amount of up to RUB500 000 (approx. EUR7 000), (ii) invalidation of the transaction in court based on an FAS claim if the FAS proves that the transaction resulted in or may result in the restriction of competition.

[330] In Russia, it is practically impossible to prevent the seller from competing with the business being sold. While including non-compete clauses in sale and purchase agreements preventing the seller from engaging in competing business is normally acceptable in other jurisdictions, in Russia the FAS has a negative position with respect to such types of non-compete restrictions, even when they are included in agreements between non-competing entities. There is no specific regulation in Russia in respect of non-compete restrictions in SPAs. In practice, the FAS generally views such clauses as leading (or potentially leading) to: (i) the division of a market by territory or by composition of buyers or customers; and/or (ii) the creation of barriers to the entry of new participants (i.e., the buyer and its affiliates) to the market. The FAS also negatively views non-compete restrictions in foreign law governed SPAs if the restrictions cover Russian territory.

[331] Non-solicitation restrictions in employment agreements are also non-enforceable in Russia. Strictly speaking, including such a non-solicitation clause in the agreement would not contravene any provision of Russian law. The court practice in this respect has not yet developed in Russia. However, if the employer refuses to employ a person relying on the non-solicitation clause, this may be viewed by the authorities as a violation of the employee's right to free employment, which is guaranteed by the Russian Constitution, as well as unjustified refusal of employment which is prohibited by Russian labour laws. Therefore, non-solicitation clauses will most likely not be enforceable in Russia. Non-competition arrangements with the employees are generally viewed as contradicting the right to free employment and are not enforceable in Russia either.

[332] Russian law does not provide for the possibility to prohibit employees from leaving the company. Therefore, the most practical approach which may be used to prevent the departure of the management team and/or key employees is providing retention bonuses for them.

[333] The FAS is the authority responsible for supervision over compliance with competition laws (including non-compete restrictions), and the Federal Labour and Employment Service (under the Ministry of Labour and Social Protection) supervises compliance with labour law.

8.2 Restrictions in 'Strategic Sectors'

[334] The most important law containing restrictions on foreign investment in specific sectors of the Russian economy is Federal Law No. 57-FZ 'On the Procedure of Making Foreign Investments in Companies of Strategic Importance for National Defense and State Security' (the '*Strategic Investments Law*'). The Strategic Investments Law lists activities which are considered to be of 'strategic importance' to Russian national defence and security. Recently, the list of such activities was expanded to forty-seven. There are plans to further revise and supplement the list of 'strategic activities'.

[335] Note that the term 'strategic activity' may be somewhat misleading. Although the list includes activities which are traditionally regarded as strategic, such as defence and security-related industries (e.g., the production of weapons, space-related activities and the operation of nuclear facilities), other non-related activities are also covered. Recently, publishing activities and/or editing or being the founder of printed media was added to the list of 'strategic activities' if the total circulation of such printed media within one year prior to the transaction or filing of an application exceeds certain thresholds. Thus, for instance, the printing of information brochures registered as mass media and issued regularly by a retailer can be viewed as 'strategic activity'.

[336] Prior approval of the Government Commission on Control over Foreign Investments in the Russian Federation (the '*Government Commission*') is mandatory for any acquisition by a foreign investor of control over a Russian company engaged in any of the forty-seven activities listed in the Strategic Investments Law (a '*Strategic Company*') or of the Strategic Company's fixed production assets the value of which constitutes 25% or more of the book value of the assets of the company.

[337] The approval must be obtained before closing the transaction. Any transactions executed without such approval are automatically null and void. The FAS may also impose a fine on the purchaser in the amount of up to RUB1 000 000 (approx. EUR15 000).

[338] The Strategic Investments Law defines the meaning of control over a Strategic Company and sets out general applicable 'control' thresholds (as well as separate (lower) thresholds applicable to Strategic Companies that use subsoil deposits of federal significance ('strategic subsoil users' or SSUs)). Foreign investors controlled by foreign states or by international organizations (so-called public foreign investors) are prohibited from acquiring control over a Strategic Company or an SSU.

Since June 2018, non-disclosing investors (i.e., those refusing to disclose to FAS information about their beneficiaries, beneficial owners and controlling persons) are subject to special, stricter regime established for public foreign investors. In December 2018, the Government approved rules for disclosure this information according to which a foreign investor planning to enter into a transaction in respect of the Strategic Company or an SSU needs to make a prior disclosure of its controlling entities, beneficiaries and beneficial owners in order to avoid being treated as a 'non-disclosing' investor and ensure that the stricter regime established for foreign public investors does not apply to it. Such disclosure has to be made either in a form of application for approval, if such approval is required, or in a form of informational letter filed with FAS thirty days before transaction.

[339] Under the Strategic Investments Law, applications have to be submitted to the FAS, which processes them (checks completeness, conducts analysis whether the target is a Strategic Company), liaises the Federal Security Service (which must provide its opinion on the impact of the planned transaction on Russian national defence and security), and involves other Government authorities (such as the Ministry of Defence and other industry-specific Ministries), as necessary. After this, the FAS refers the application to the Government Commission for further review and approval.

[340] The Strategic Investments Law does not apply to (i) transactions involving a Strategic Company where the acquirer is an entity ultimately controlled by the Russian Federation or its constituent entity or by a Russian citizen being a tax resident of the Russian Federation and not having other citizenship, (ii) transactions with respect to SSUs where the Russian Federation has the right to dispose of, directly or indirectly, more than 50% of voting shares (participatory interests) in the SSU before the transaction and will retain this right after the transaction's completion (this exemption, however, will not apply if the transaction is performed by a public foreign investor); and (iii) certain intra-group transactions with respect to Strategic Companies of SSUs. In its clarifications to the Strategic Investments Law FAS emphasized that the abovementioned requirement to disclose information on the acquirer's beneficiaries, beneficial owners and controlling persons extends to transactions exempted under item (i) above, and is a pre-requisite for the relevant exemption being applicable.

[341] The statutory period for the application review under the Strategic Investments Law is three months from the date when the FAS accepted the application until the date when the official decision on the application is issued (the FAS is responsible for printing and issuing official decisions based on the results of the Government Commission's meeting). This three-month period may be extended for an additional three months in exceptional cases by the decision of the Government Commission. In practice, the Government Commission may meet infrequently (two to three times per year) and, as a result, the necessity to obtain the prior approval of the Government Commission may have a significant impact on the timeline of the transaction.

[342] Another important law governing foreign investments in Russia is Federal Law No. 160-FZ 'On Foreign Investments in the Russian Federation' (the '*Foreign Investments Law*'). The Foreign Investments Law establishes further restrictions that apply to 'public' foreign investors. Pursuant to the Foreign Investments Law, prior approval is mandatory for acquisitions by 'public' investors of more than 25% of the voting shares in (or blocking rights with respect to) any Russian company, whether such company is a Strategic Company or not.

[343] Although the contents of filings relating to public foreign investors are subject to the Strategic Investments Law requirements as to scope and format of documents, they must be prepared as part of a separate procedure. Similar to the applications submitted under the Strategic Investments Law, such applications must also be made with and processed by the FAS. However, filings made under the Foreign Investments Law are approved by the FAS, without the need to refer the matter to the Government Commission (unless the FAS determines that the target company is a Strategic Company or that, due to the target's access to the top secret information, the application should be filed to and reviewed by the Government Commission). Approvals under the Foreign Investments Law are usually issued within thirty calendar days after the filing of the application.

Amendments to the Foreign Investments Law introduced in 2017 gave the Chairman of the Government Commission the right to decide that a prior approval is required with respect to any transaction by any foreign investor with regard to any Russian company, if this is needed for the purpose of ensuring national defense and state security. Upon receipt of such a decision from the Government Commission, FAS will notify the foreign investor about the need to receive approval for a prospective transaction. Any transaction made in breach of this requirement is void. The practice on the type of transactions that could potentially fall under the requirements of this amendment is still being formed. FAS in its clarifications confirmed that in practice this rule so far has been applied to very exclusive cases only.

[344] The approval must be obtained before closing of the transaction. The FAS may impose a fine on the purchaser in the amount of up to RUB1 000 000 (approx. EUR15 000). In addition, the FAS may request a court to invalidate the transaction if it violates Russian law.

[345] Since 2011, certain international financial organizations (IFOs) are exempt from the requirement to obtain clearance under the Strategic Investments Law and the Foreign Investments Law. A list of exempted IFOs was approved by the Russian government and it includes the EBRD, IFC, the International Bank for Reconstruction and Development, and other major IFOs.

8.3 Industry Specific Restrictions on Foreign Investments in Russia

[346] The Foreign Investments Law[88] grants certain privileges and protections to 'commercial organizations with foreign investments' and these include all companies with a foreign participant, regardless of the size of the foreign participant's shareholding in the company. On the other hand, Russian law may impose restrictions on companies with foreign ownership depending on the industry and statutory sensitivity of investments. Some examples are listed below.

8.4 Restrictions in the Insurance Sector

[347] The acquisition of participation in a Russian insurance company by a foreign investor is subject to the following restrictions.

[348] *Insurance as the investor's main activity:* A foreign investor may acquire a 49% or greater participation interest in a Russian insurance company only if it has been conducting insurance business in its country of incorporation for at least five years.

[349] *Quota for foreign* participation *in the charter capital of all Russian insurance companies:* Russian law establishes a maximum quota of 50% for the participation of foreign capital in the charter capital of all Russian insurance companies. If the quota is used up (or will be used up after a particular acquisition), the Central Bank may refuse to grant its consent. The actual quota is calculated annually. As of 1 January 2019, the actual quota was 11.99%.[89]

[88] Federal Law No. 160-FZ On Foreign Investments in the Russian Federation, dated 9 July 1999 (as amended) (the '*Foreign Investments Law*').

[89] Information letter of the Central Bank, dated 28 February 2019.

[350] Central *Bank consent for foreign participation in a Russian insurance company:* The Central Bank's prior consent is required for Russian participants/shareholders of a Russian insurance company in order to sell their participatory interests/shares to a foreign investor or its subsidiary; and the Russian insurance company must obtain Central Bank's consent prior to increasing its charter capital with the foreign investor's funds. In this context, a foreign investor is defined as a foreign organization that has the right to invest according to the procedures and terms established by Russian law in the charter capital of Russian insurance companies being established or already established. A company is deemed to be a subsidiary if another (i.e., main) company, based on the prevailing participation in the charter capital or agreement existing between such companies or otherwise, has an opportunity to determine resolutions made by the subsidiary company. The statutory term for the issuance of Central Bank consent is thirty calendar days.

[351] The Central Bank may go to court to challenge a foreign investor's acquisition of a participation interest in a Russian insurance company without the Central Bank's consent.

8.5 Restrictions in the Banking Sector

[352] The establishment and acquisition of a participation interest in a Russian credit organization by a foreign investor are subject to the following restrictions.

[353] *Quota for foreign participation in the charter capital of Russian credit organizations:* Russian banking regulations place a 50% limit on the level of foreign participation in the aggregate charter capital of Russian credit organizations (quota). If this quota is achieved, the Central Bank will: (i) refuse to register new credit organizations with foreign investments or grant such credit organizations a banking license; and (ii) impose a ban on transfer of shares in the Russian credit organizations to the foreign investors and prohibit the increase of the charter capital of credit organizations by way of contributions by foreign shareholders (given that the respective transfer or charter capital increase will result in exceeding the quota).

[354] As of 1 January 2019, the size of foreign investor participation in the aggregate charter capital of Russian credit organizations was 12.41%,[90] which is significantly below the established limit.

[355] *Central Bank consent for acquisition of participation in a Russian credit organization:* Any direct or indirect acquisition of more than 10% of the shares in a Russian bank requires prior approval by the Central Bank.

[90] Information of the Central Bank dated 15 February 2019 (https://www.cbr.ru/press/event/?id=2420).

8.6 Restrictions in the Aviation Sector

[356] In the aviation sector, the major restriction relates to foreign shareholding in an aviation organization conducting air transportation activities in Russia. Specifically, foreign participation in the charter capital of an aviation organization may not exceed 49%.

8.7 Restrictions in the Mass Media

[357] Unless an international treaty to which Russia is a party provides otherwise, a foreign investor may not:

- directly establish or participate in a Russian mass media enterprise (i.e., a mass media company, editors of mass media and legal entities engaged in broadcasting);
- own, manage or control directly or indirectly (including through entities under their control or by owning more than 20% of stock (shares) of any type) more than 20% of the stock (shares) in the charter capital of the participant (member or shareholder) of the founder of mass media enterprise;[91]
- establish any other forms of control resulting in the direct or indirect ownership, management, control or actual determination of decisions adopted by the mass media enterprise and its founders.

[358] All transactions resulting in breach of the above-mentioned requirements are void.

[359] If they do not comply with the above requirements, the participants (founders) of a mass media enterprise's founder will not be able to exercise their corporate rights provided for in the Civil Code (such as participating in the management of the company, receiving information about its operations, reviewing its accounting documents, appealing the decisions of its bodies, requesting indemnification of damage caused to the company, challenging transactions).

8.8 Restrictions in Land Legislation

[360] Foreign investors are not allowed to own certain categories of land in Russia. In particular, foreign investors are prohibited from acquiring land located (i) in areas close to national borders[92] and (ii) other territories specifically set out by the federal laws (e.g., foreign investors or companies in which foreign ownership of the charter capital exceeds 50% may only enjoy lease rights to agricultural land).

[91] With regard to Russian legal entities with foreign capital, this limitation applies to the Russian legal entities with more than 20% of foreign capital in their charter capital.

[92] A list of such areas is approved by Decree No. 26 of the Russian President dated 9 January 2011.

9 ROLE OF COURTS

9.1 General Considerations

[361] Since Russia is a civil law jurisdiction, case law formally does not constitute a source of law. However, the Constitutional Court decisions interpreting the Constitution are binding for Russian courts. Importantly, commercial courts are obliged to follow the Supreme Court's and the former Supreme Commercial Court's legal positions as stipulated by law.

[362] In particular, the resolutions of the Plenum of the Supreme Court and the effective resolutions of the former Plenum of the Supreme Commercial Court are binding for Russian courts. The resolutions of the Plenum of the Supreme Court and the resolutions of the Presidium of the Supreme Court changing the current case law could be used as a basis for the reconsideration of a court decision that has become legally binding, where these resolutions provide for the possibility to do so. The Supreme Court summarizes case law and issues court practice explanations in the form of overviews (the former Supreme Commercial Court also issued information letters). Such explanations are used as interpretative recommendations and guidelines for lower courts when dealing with similar issues. [93]

[363] Enforcement of contractual and other rights through the courts is relatively efficient in Russia.[94] Although the duration of the proceedings depends on the judge's abilities and his/her workload, certain time standards set by law make case management in Russia relatively fast.

[364] Russian law provides for specific time limits for consideration of cases by commercial courts and courts of general jurisdiction. In commercial procedure, the Courts of First Instance are required to consider a case within six months from receiving the statement of claim. This time limit may be extended to nine months. In civil procedure, as a rule, the courts are required to consider a case within two months from receiving the statement of claim. This time limit may be extended for a month. If the court appoints an expert, or sends a request for legal assistance, it may suspend the proceedings until completion of these actions. However, the

[93] Determination or change of the interpretation of a legal norm by a resolution of the Plenum of the Supreme Court or resolution of the Presidium of the Supreme Court, if the relevant decision of the Supreme Court specifies the possibility of review of effective court decisions by virtue of this occurrence, serves as a ground for the review of lower court decisions due to new facts (Art. 311(3)(5) of the Commercial Procedure Code). The reasoning of court decisions may contain references to resolutions of the Plenum of the Supreme Court and the effective resolutions of the Plenum of the former Supreme Commercial Court on issues of judicial interpretation. It may also contain references to resolutions of the Presidium of the Supreme Court, the resolutions of the former Presidium of the Supreme Commercial Court which remain in effect, and the Overviews of court practice adopted by the Presidium of the Supreme Court (Art. 170(4)(3) of the Commercial Procedure Code).

[94] According to the World Bank's survey 'Doing Business 2020' on enforcement of commercial contracts, Russia's *Quality of judicial processes index* is relatively high – 9.5 out of a possible score of 18. It is ranked 21st out of 190 economies on the ease of enforcing contracts and its distance to frontier measure is 72.2 % (*See*: https://www.doingbusiness.org/en/data/exploreeconomies/russia#DB_ec).

courts are required to consider cases in a reasonable time and a party may request the chief judge to accelerate the court proceedings.

[365] The availability of electronic filing and electronic case management increases the efficiency of commercial courts. Some options for electronic case management are also available in courts of general jurisdiction. Court judgments (and procedural rulings) in commercial cases are published in a database on the website of the Supreme Commercial Court (http://kad.arbitr.ru/). Court judgments in civil cases are published in an anonymized manner (i.e., without details of the parties) on the websites of the courts of general jurisdiction of a particular region of the Russian Federation (e.g., Moscow City Court in Moscow).

[366] Foreign citizens and legal entities may sue and be sued in Russian courts in the same way as Russian citizens and legal entities. If the claimant or respondent is a foreign national or foreign legal entity, it must file evidence of its nationality, legal form, capacity and information regarding its authorized representatives (e.g., a statement from the relevant trade register). The date of this statement must not be earlier than thirty days before the date of filing of the statement of claim with the court. If a document must be apostilled, the claimant must receive the document within a reasonable time before filing the statement of claim, and have it apostilled within thirty days before filing the statement of claim with the court. Any documents in a foreign language must be translated into Russian. The translation must be certified by a Russian notary or Russian consular agent, unless an international agreement provides otherwise.[95]

[367] It should be noted that the judiciary in Russia may lack experience in adjudicating complex commercial cases. Independence and efficiency of the judges may be a cause for concern.[96]

9.2 Judicial Reform

[368] The reform of the Russian judicial system started in 2014. The aim of the reform was to ensure a uniform approach to dispute resolution by commercial courts and courts of general jurisdiction and to avoid disputes on jurisdiction. The reform abolished the Supreme Commercial Court and transferred its supervisory functions to the Supreme Court. The newly established Supreme Court started considering commercial disputes from 6 August 2014. The system of Commercial Courts of First Instance, as well as circuit commercial courts of the appellate and

[95] For example, under Art. 6 of the Agreement between the Commonwealth of Independent States (CIS) states on the procedure for resolution of disputes related to commercial activities dated 20 March 1992, documents issued or certified by authorities of a member state are accepted in other member states without any additional certification.

[96] Russia is ranked 88th out of 126 countries in the Rule of Law Index for civil justice, 2019 (*See*: https://worldjusticeproject.org/our-work/research-and-data/wjp-rule-law-index-2019).

cassation instances, remained unchanged. The system of courts of general jurisdiction was reformed in 2019. In particular, separate cassation courts of general jurisdiction were introduced similar to the commercial court model, with further harmonization of procedural law.

[369] Starting from 6 August 2014, the Supreme Court became a supervising authority for commercial courts. As a result, second-level cassation appeals may be filed with the Economic Division of the Supreme Court and may be considered, provided that leave for appeal is granted. Decisions of the Economic Division may be further appealed to the Presidium of the Supreme Court.

[370] Importantly, the Economic Division rulings often cite the Supreme Commercial Court's 'heritage', i.e., the legal positions formulated in the resolutions of the Plenum of the Supreme Commercial Court and the resolutions and information fetters of the Presidium of the Supreme Commercial Court. While the number of 'precedent-setting' decisions and important legal positions in the rulings of the Economic Division has decreased, only in a few cases has the Economic Division departed from the legal positions previously developed by the Supreme Commercial Court.

9.3 Arbitration Reform

[371] Russian law recognizes arbitration (domestic arbitration) as a way of resolving disputes. In December 2015, Russian arbitration legislation underwent substantial amendments.[97] Such amendments were adopted with a view to promoting efficient arbitration in Russia with a special emphasis on institutional arbitration, to combat 'pocket' domestic arbitration institutions and various schemes, in particular, aimed at tax avoidance, money laundering, creation of artificial debts, and legalization of assets. The purpose of the reform was also to reduce the number and improve the quality of domestic arbitration institutions, and to harmonize the regulation of international and domestic arbitration.

[372] The new rules required the permanent arbitration institutions handling Russian-seated proceedings to obtain a special permit (license) from the Government by 1 November 2017. There were only two exceptions: the International Commercial Arbitration Court (ICAC) and the Maritime Arbitration Commission (MAC) at the Chamber of Commerce and Industry of the Russian Federation that did not need to obtain such authorization. Permits can be issued upon the recommendation of a special Council for Development of Arbitration established by the Ministry of Justice specifically for this purpose. To comply with a number of law requirements, arbitration institutions had to change their internal procedures and arbitration rules. As a result, the arbitration institutions which obtained permits are (i) the Arbitration Center at the all-Russian non-profit organization 'Russian Union of Industrialists and Entrepreneurs', (ii) the Russian Arbitration Center at the

[97] Federal Laws No. 382-FZ 'On Arbitration (domestic arbitration) in the Russian Federation' and No. 409-FZ 'On amendments to certain legislative acts' dated 29 December 2015.

Autonomous non-profit organization 'Russian Institute of Modern Arbitration', and (iii) the National Center for Sports Arbitration at the Autonomous non-profit organization 'Sports Arbitration Chamber'. The international arbitration institutions that have obtained state authorization to administer arbitrations are: (i) the Hong Kong International Arbitration Centre (HKIAC) and (ii) the Vienna International Arbitral Centre (VIAC). Permanent arbitration institutions have important advantages compared to *ad hoc* arbitration. In particular, only permanent arbitration institutions can handle corporate cases (except for non-arbitral corporate disputes).

[373] The reform also addressed the form of an arbitration agreement. The new rules provide that arbitration clauses can be agreed in electronic form. They can be contained in the corporate (shareholders') agreements and articles of association of a company, except for public joint stock companies and companies having more than 1 000 shareholders with voting rights.[98] The Plenum of the Supreme Court clarified that when a new shareholder acquires shares, he/she is taken to give consent to be bound by the arbitration agreement contained in the articles of association, unless the articles of association provide otherwise.[99] Furthermore, doubts regarding the validity of arbitration clauses should be interpreted in favour of their validity and enforcement.[100] The Plenum of the Supreme Court explained that a party who challenges the validity and/or enforceability of the arbitration agreement has to prove that all of the possible interpretations of the arbitration agreement led to its invalidity and/or unenforceability.[101]

[374] The new rules also stipulate that certain issues may be agreed only by way of 'express agreement' of the parties, meaning that to be valid the parties' agreement on such issues must be expressly set out in the text of the parties' arbitration clause, rather than addressed in the arbitration rules to which the arbitration clause refers. Issues which may be addressed only by the parties' 'express agreement' include, in particular, excluding the possibility of setting aside the final award.

9.4 Arbitrability of Corporate Disputes

[375] The rules concerning the arbitrability of corporate disputes resolve the ambiguity over the arbitrability of various types of corporate disputes which has

98 Article 7(8) of the Law No. 5338-1 'On International Commercial Arbitration' dated 7 July 1993; Article 7(7) of the Federal Law No. 382-FZ 'On Arbitration in the Russian Federation' dated 29 December 2015 (the 'Arbitration Law').

99 Clause 23, Resolution of the Plenum of the Supreme Court of the Russian Federation No. 53 'On the fulfilment by the courts of the Russian Federation of the functions of assistance and control in relation to arbitration, including international commercial arbitration' dated 10 December 2019.

100 Article 7(9) of the Law No. 5338-1 'On International Commercial Arbitration' dated 7 July 1993; Art. 7(8) of the Arbitration Law.

101 Clause 26, Resolution of the Plenum of the Supreme Court of the Russian Federation No. 53 'On the fulfilment by the courts of the Russian Federation of the functions of assistance and control in relation to arbitration, including international commercial arbitration' dated 10 December 2019.

existed for several years and introduce a relatively clear-cut set of solutions. Corporate disputes for this purpose include any disputes in connection with the participation in, or management of, Russian companies, including any disputes relating to the ownership of shares in Russian companies. The rules distinguish between non-arbitrable corporate disputes and corporate disputes arbitrable in institutional arbitration seated in Russia.

[376] Non-arbitrable corporate disputes are those relating to/arising out of:

- convening general shareholders' meetings;
- exclusion of shareholders;
- challenging resolutions and actions of state authorities with respect to the issuance of stock; and
- strategic legal entities (except where the amount of shares in dispute does not exceed the threshold which triggers the need to obtain approval from the Government Commission on Monitoring Foreign Investment).

[377] Corporate disputes arbitrable in institutional arbitration seated in Russia and resolved under special arbitration rules for corporate disputes, provided that the company itself, all of its shareholders, and any other persons acting as claimants or defendants are parties to the arbitration agreement. These are disputes relating to/arising out of:

- challenging transactions performed by the legal entity;
- corporate (shareholders') agreements regarding a company's management;
- establishment, reorganization and liquidation of legal entities;
- challenging the resolutions of management bodies; and
- appointment/election and removal of directors and their liability.

[378] Corporate disputes arbitrable in institutional arbitration not necessarily seated in Russia and in the absence of special rules for corporate disputes. These are disputes relating to/arising out of:

- ownership of shares and enforcement of share pledge agreements; and
- activity of registrars.

[379] The rules concerning the arbitrability of corporate disputes entered into force on 1 September 2016, although a number of provisions took effect later. Starting from 1 February 2017, it has become possible to enter into an arbitration agreement which refers to the above types of corporate disputes to arbitration.

[380] The amendments to the Arbitration Law were introduced on 27 December 2018 (in force as of 29 March 2019).[102] They simplified the requirements for arbitrability of two types of the above disputes: (1) challenging transactions performed by a company, and (2) disputes arising out of a corporate (shareholders') agreement regarding a company's management. Starting from 29 March 2019, in order for these disputes to be arbitrable an arbitration agreement between the parties to a shareholders' agreement or a transaction (irrespective of express consent of a

[102] Federal Law No. 531-FZ 'On the Incorporation of Amendments to the Federal Law On Arbitration in the Russian Federation and to the Federal Law On Advertising' dated 27 December 2018.

'third party' to be bound by an arbitration agreement) is sufficient. In addition, disputes arising out of a corporate (shareholders') agreement can be heard in institutional arbitration in the absence of special arbitration rules for corporate disputes. However, these amendments do not provide any guidance on whether the seat of arbitration can be located outside the Russian Federation.[103] By contrast, the rules of the Commercial Procedure Code remain unchanged[104] and require that the seat of arbitration must be in Russia. Therefore, in our view, the amendments to the Arbitration Law, as more recent and special rules, prevail over the Commercial Procedure Code provisions, except for the rules governing the seat of arbitration (which remain effective).

[381] It should be noted that Russian law does not allow disputes arising out of SPAs or option agreements to be referred to an international arbitration institution with the seat of arbitration in Russia if such international arbitration institution has not received a permit of the Russian Federation. At the same time, under Russian law, it is not clear whether an international arbitration institution needs a permit of the Government of the Russian Federation to resolve share title disputes where the seat of the arbitration is outside the Russian Federation. The amendments do not expressly answer this question and there is a high risk that the Russian courts will hold awards rendered in such arbitration unenforceable.

9.5 Protection of Minority Shareholders in Court

[382] Pursuant to the JSC Law and the clarifications of the Supreme Court in its 'Overview of court practice on certain issues related to application of corporate law', dated 25 December 2019, all minority shareholders have the right to defend their interests through court proceedings and bring claims against other shareholders and top management in the cases listed below. Each minority shareholder, irrespective of the stake, has the right:

- to challenge a transaction which was made without proper corporate approval (including major transactions and interested party transactions); this transaction may be challenged despite the fact that it caused no damages to the company;
- to challenge a decision of a general shareholders' meeting (if he/she did not participate in such meeting, in particular, because he/she was not duly notified of such meeting, or voted against the relevant item of the agenda) referring to the fact that the decision violates Russian law or the charter and adversely affects the shareholder's legitimate interests; a decision of a general shareholders' meeting on increasing the charter capital may be challenged if such decision fails to meet

[103] Articles 7(7.1), 45(7.1) of the Arbitration Law.

[104] Article 225.1(4) of the Commercial Procedure Code provides that these types of disputes may be referred to arbitration only if all shareholders of the company and all claimants and respondents are parties to the arbitration agreement. Art. 225.1(3) of the Commercial Procedure Code provides that disputes arising out of a corporate (shareholders') agreement can be resolved only by institutional arbitration seated in Russia and under special arbitration rules for corporate disputes.

the company's interests and results in a dilution of a share of a minority shareholder who voted against such decision; a decision of a general shareholders' meeting may also be challenged if it contradicts the company's and/or the minority shareholder's interests, and the shareholder who contributed to the adoption of such decision was acting for his/her own benefit or in bad faith.
- to challenge a resolution of the board of directors referring to the fact that the decision violates Russian law or the charter and adversely affects the shareholder's legitimate interests;
- to request a court to order the expulsion of other shareholders from the company if by their actions or omissions they caused substantial damage to the company; availability of other remedies, for example, recovery of damages caused by such actions or omissions, may not affect this right;
- to seek either (i) restoration of his/her status as a shareholder by claiming his/her shares back, or (ii) compensation for lost shares (if such loss occurred as a result of illegal actions of other shareholders or third parties); and
- to bring an action against top management of the company and demand compensation for damage suffered due to their misconduct.

[383] Minority shareholders owning in aggregate *not less than 1% of shares* enjoy an additional right to bring a class action suit against top management of the company and demand compensation of damage incurred by the company due to their misconduct.

[384] A shareholder who challenges a decision of a general shareholders' meeting or claims restitution for losses from a manager or member of the board, or challenges a transaction (or demands that a transaction be deemed invalid) must take all reasonable measures to inform the other shareholders of the company of his/her intention to file a claim in court. For this purpose, he/she must provide the company with a written notification of such intention that must be received by the company at least five days before filing a claim. The company must inform its shareholders about such notification not later than three days after the court allows the claim. The procedure of notification of the shareholders differs for non-public and public companies. Non-public companies must inform their shareholders in the same order as stipulated by law for convening general shareholders' meetings unless otherwise provided by the company's articles of association. Public companies must publish a notification on the website that is used for disclosure and disclose such information in the same order as the legal regulations require for disclosure of notices of material facts.

[385] If the other shareholders do not support the claim (following the rules of procedure), they lose the right to bring a court action for identical claims, unless the court acknowledges the legitimacy of the underlying reasons for bringing a separate action.

9.6 Governing Law and Dispute Resolution

[386] The choice of law to apply to an agreement will depend on the following considerations:

- Are the parties free to choose any law to apply to the agreement?
- May the parties refer disputes under the agreement to any international arbitration institute located outside Russia (e.g., the London Court of International Arbitration, International Chamber of Commerce (Paris) or Stockholm Chamber of Commerce)? If not, does it make sense to apply non-Russian law to the relevant agreement?

[387] Generally, parties to a contract may choose a foreign law as the governing law of the contract and they may refer certain types of disputes to international arbitration. The choice of foreign law in respect of a contract shall be valid and effective under Russian law provided that at least one party to a contract is a foreign entity, or the respective legal relationship involves some other foreign element (e.g., the contract is performed outside of Russia or involves a Russian asset). By contrast, if there is no sufficient foreign element ('if all circumstances relating to the substance of the contractual relations were connected to only one country'), the choice of foreign law shall not affect any mandatory rules of the jurisdiction with which the contract was genuinely connected.[105] This means that any mandatory Russian law rules would apply in this case regardless of the choice of foreign law.

[388] The application of foreign law may not contradict overriding mandatory provisions (rules of immediate application).[106] Russian law distinguishes between 'regular' mandatory rules (which can be replaced by foreign law provided there is a sufficient foreign element) and overriding mandatory provisions (which apply regardless of the choice of law). There is no list of overriding mandatory provisions under Russian law. They are either expressly designated as such by federal laws or identified by courts. By way of example, an overriding mandatory provision is the prohibition for foreign entities to acquire shareholding in certain 'strategic' Russian entities (e.g., in a Russian company producing engines for the Russian military).[107]

[389] Under Russian law, the choice of governing law in shareholders' agreements must observe not only 'overriding', but also 'regular' mandatory Russian law rules applicable to internal relations in Russian companies, including relations between the company and its shareholders.[108] Therefore, it is questionable whether, for example, it makes sense to subject shareholders' agreements to a foreign law in a situation where mandatory Russian law rules will still need to be observed.

[105] Article 1210(5) of the Civil Code; Clause 32 of the Resolution of the Plenum of the Russian Supreme Court No. 24 dated 9 July 2019.

[106] Article 1192 of the Civil Code.

[107] Clause 10 of the Resolution of the Plenum of the Supreme Court No. 24 dated 9 July 2019.

[108] Article 1214(1) of the Civil Code.

[390] A Russian court will not apply foreign law provisions which are in conflict with the '*public policy*' of the Russian Federation.[109] The public policy principle means that a rule of foreign law will not be applied in 'exceptional cases' when its application would result in violation of the 'fundamental principles of the Russian legal system', and that such a violation may damage sovereignty or national security, affect the interests of large social groups, or infringe the constitutional rights and freedoms of individuals or legal entities.[110]

[391] It should be noted that if the Russian court is not able to ascertain the contents of the relevant law chosen by the parties within a reasonable time, it shall apply Russian law.[111]

[392] Furthermore, any agreement should be made in the language of the jurisdiction whose laws govern the agreement. This will ensure that, in the event of dispute, it is easy for a court or arbitration tribunal to interpret the agreement and the intent of the parties set out therein. If an agreement is made in two languages, it is highly recommended that one of those languages be the language of the governing law and that the agreement contains a clause indicating that in the event of any conflict or discrepancy the language of the governing law prevails.

[393] The rules on arbitrability need be followed so that any award would be enforceable both in Russia and in any country which is a party to the New York Convention.

9.7 Enforceability of Foreign Court Decisions and Arbitration Awards in Russia

[394] Pursuant to the provisions of the Commercial Procedure Code, decisions of foreign courts are recognized and enforced in Russia only if there is an international treaty or a Russian federal law which directly provides for such enforcement and recognition.[112] It should be noted that most foreign countries (including the US and the United Kingdom) do not have treaties on the enforcement of court judgments with Russia.[113] In the absence of such international treaties, Russian

[109] Clause 12 of the Resolution of the Plenum of the Russian Supreme Court No. 24 dated 9 July 2019.

[110] Clause 51 of the Resolution of the Plenum of the Russian Supreme Court.

[111] Article 1191(3) of the Civil Code.

[112] Article 241(1) of the 'Commercial Procedure Code of the Russian Federation' No. 95-FZ dated 24.07.2002 (the *'Commercial Procedure Code'*). According to Art. 241(1), foreign court decisions issued in disputes and other cases arising out of the performance of entrepreneurial and other economic activities (*foreign court decisions*), awards issued by arbitral tribunals and international commercial arbitration courts in foreign states in disputes and other matters arising out of the performance of entrepreneurial and other economic activities (*foreign arbitration awards*) would be recognized and enforced by commercial courts in the Russian Federation if the recognition and enforcement of such decisions is provided for by an international treaty to which the Russian Federation is a party, and the federal law. Although the wording of the law is not clear, it is sufficient to have either an international treaty or a federal law to enforce a foreign judgment, and not necessarily both.

[113] Most international treaties were entered into with the former Soviet Union countries, such as the Republic of Belarus, Turkmenistan, etc.

courts may recognize and enforce foreign judgments on the basis of (i) other relevant international treaties[114] and (ii) the principles of international comity and reciprocity.

[395] On the basis of comity and reciprocity, the Russian commercial courts recognized and/or enforced, *inter alia*, judgments rendered in the following countries: the UK,[115] the Netherlands,[116] Denmark,[117] Belgium,[118] British Virgin Islands,[119] and the US.[120] However, the principles of comity and reciprocity are not always followed by the Russian courts. By way of example, a Russian court refused to recognize and enforce a US judgment concluding, *inter alia*, that there was no evidence of mutual recognition and enforcement between Russia and the US.[121] This is despite the fact that there has been at least one US judgment enforced in Russia.

[396] In contrast to foreign court decisions, foreign arbitral awards may be enforced in Russia pursuant to the terms of the Convention on the Recognition and Enforcement of Foreign Arbitral Awards (the '*New York Convention*')[122] to which Russia is a party.

[397] The list of grounds for denial of recognition and enforcement of a foreign arbitral award is exhaustive and based on the relevant provisions of the New York Convention. The relevant grounds include the following:

- a party lacked capacity under applicable law or the agreement to arbitrate was invalid;
- a party was not given proper notification of the arbitration proceedings;

[114] By way of example, the Supreme Commercial Court recognised a judgment of the High Court of Justice of Northern Ireland on the basis of 2003 UN Convention against Corruption, 1994 Partnership and Cooperation Agreement between the European Communities and Russia, 1992 UK-Russia Economic Co-operation Agreement and 1950 European Convention on Human Rights (Resolution of the Presidium of the Supreme Commercial Court No. 6004/13 dated 8 October 2013).

[115] *See, e.g.*, Resolution of the Commercial Court of the Moscow Circuit No. F05-13737/2014 dated 28 September 2015 and Resolution of the Federal Commercial Court of the Moscow Circuit No. A41-32587/14 dated 17 August 2015.

[116] *See* Resolution of the Commercial Court of the Moscow Circuit No. A41-9613/09 dated 29 July 2009 and Resolution of the Commercial Court of the Povolzhye Circuit No. A55-5718/2011 dated 23 January 2012.

[117] *See* Ruling of the Commercial Court of the City of Saint-Petersburg and Leningrad Region in Case No. A56-56528/2005 dated 22 February 2006.

[118] *See* Ruling of the Commercial Court of the City of Moscow in Case No. A40-59094/2013 dated 30 August 2013 (affirmed by the cassation court in part).

[119] *See, e.g.*, Ruling of the Commercial Court of the City of Moscow in Case No. A40-176337/2014 dated 10 March 2015, Ruling of the Commercial Court of the City of Moscow in Case No. A40-186882/2017 dated 12 December 2017.

[120] Ruling of the Commercial Court of the City of Moscow in Case No. A40-99438/2011 dated 1 December 2011.

[121] Resolution of the Commercial Court of the Moscow Circuit No. F05-15556/2017 dated 19 October 2017.

[122] The Convention on the Recognition and Enforcement of Foreign Arbitral Awards entered into in New York on 10 June 1958 (came into force on 7 June 1959).

- the arbitration was not conducted in accordance with the arbitration agreement or, in the absence of such agreement, the law of the country where the arbitration took place;
- the award addressed matters beyond the scope of the agreement to arbitrate;
- the subject matter of the dispute was not capable of settlement by arbitration in the Russian Federation;
- the award has not become binding on the parties, or has been set aside or suspended; or
- the recognition and enforcement of the award would violate public policy of the Russian Federation.

[398] Foreign arbitral awards are enforced in Russia through an application to the state courts. Given the relative ease with which international arbitration awards can be enforced in Russia, in most cross-border M&A transactions on the Russian market, the parties may refer their disputes to international arbitration institutions authorized to operate in Russia (HKIAC and VIAC).

[399] There is, however, a concern that the Russian courts sometimes interpret the concept of public policy rather expansively. According to the Russian Arbitration Association's statistical analysis of the Russian case law on enforcement of foreign arbitral awards (2008–2017),[123] the courts found that enforcement of awards would be contrary to the Russian public policy in 39% cases (twenty cases out of fifty-one cases where public policy ground was invoked). In 2013, the Supreme Commercial Court adopted the Overview on application of the public policy concept. As a result, the number of court granted public policy motions dropped to nil in the following years. Its effect lasted until 2017 when the public policy argument regained its popularity (the rate of refusals on the public policy ground rose to 92% (eleven cases out of twelve)). In 2019, the Plenum of the Supreme Court remarked, in line with the Supreme Commercial Court's earlier position, that the public policy ground was to be invoked only in extraordinary circumstances. The effect of this clarification is yet to be seen.

10 TAXATION ASPECTS

10.1 Nature of Taxation Regime

[400] The Russian taxation system is regulated by the Tax Code (the federal law consisting of two parts: Part One (in effect from 1999), which defines the general taxation principles, the types of taxes and tax regimes, the scope of rights and obligations of the tax authorities and taxpayers, and tax fines, and Part Two, which combines currently twenty-one chapters dedicated to particular types of taxes and tax regimes), as well as by regional laws of the constituent entities of the Russian

[123] https://arbitration.ru/upload/iblock/88d/RAA-STUDY-RECOGNITION-ENFORCEMENT-AWARDS-NY-CONVENTION-2018_eng.pdf

Federation and normative acts of municipalities adopted in accordance with the Tax Code. The rules established in the Tax Code are directly applicable, save for specific aspects whose regulation is assigned to state authorities. International treaties on tax matters have priority over the Russian tax laws and, once ratified, apply directly, subject to procedural rules and requirements set forth in the Tax Code.

[401] The principles and procedural rules of tax administration and tax audits are explicitly defined in the Tax Code and usually observed by the tax authorities in practice. As a general rule, the tax authorities can audit a taxpayer's results for the three preceding calendar years. Additional tax assessments may be disputed by taxpayers in administrative proceedings and then in court; usually such proceedings are completed within a year.

10.2 Tax Liability

[402] For corporate capital gains tax purposes, the Russian tax residency rules apply based on a dual principle: (i) any legal entity incorporated in Russia is recognized as a Russian tax resident; and (ii) a legal entity incorporated outside of Russia is recognized as Russian tax resident if it has a place of management in Russia. The place of management is considered to be in Russia if (a) the executive body(ies) regularly performs its(their) functions in Russia; or (b) the senior officials (responsible for management, planning and control) perform their functions predominantly in Russia. Additional determining factors include: (i) the place where accounting records are prepared; (ii) the place where record-keeping functions are performed; and (iii) the place where operative HR management takes place. If these conditions are met, the foreign legal entity may file a notification on self-election of Russian tax residence status (such filing presumes, however, that the foreign legal entity has a Russian branch or representative office). The positive effect for the foreign legal entity from establishing Russian tax residence includes the entitlement to the participation exemption with regard to dividends (*see* paragraph. [407]) and the exclusion from controlled foreign company (CFC) taxation (*see* paragraph [412]).

[403] A number of categories of foreign legal entities are excluded from the Russian tax residence rules. For the following types of foreign legal entities, Russian tax residence arises only by self-election: (i) mining project participants; (ii) operators of new offshore hydrocarbon fields; (iii) active CFCs (for these categories – under the same conditions as they qualify for the tax exemption under the CFC rules, *see* paragraph [411]); and (iv) entities engaged in (sub)lease of sea vessels or international transportation of goods or passengers. The following types of foreign legal entities are safeguarded from the need to establish Russian tax residence altogether: (i) entities that perform their activities with their own qualified personnel and assets located in a treaty country (or in a treaty country where it has a subdivision); and (ii) bond issuers (under the same conditions as they qualify for the tax exemption under the CFC rules, *see* paragraph [411]).

[404] Legal entities that are recognized as Russian tax residents are subject to Russian corporate income tax on their world-wide income, subject to a limited foreign tax credit (however, with regard to dividend income only if the tax credit is provided for under the treaty).

[405] Legal entities that are not recognized as Russian tax residents may be taxed in Russia on their active income derived through a permanent establishment and on their passive income (*see* paragraph [412]).

[406] Under the general taxation regime, the following taxes apply to Russian tax-resident legal entities and permanent establishments of non-resident legal entities: (i) corporate profit tax (standard rate of 20%); (ii) VAT (standard rate of 20% (18% – before 2019) for domestic sales and 0% for export sales); (iii) additional tax for mining companies (mineral extraction tax and additional income tax on carbon extraction); (iv) taxes on corporate property: property tax, transport vehicle tax and land tax; (v) taxes on employment: income tax (to be withheld from employees) and social security contributions; (vi) customs duties on the import and export of goods; (vii) excise tax on the production, sale and import of certain categories of goods; and (viii) stamp duties for certain actions performed by the state authorities and notaries.

[407] Dividend income received by tax resident companies is subject to corporate profit tax at the rate of 13%. There is an exemption for dividends received based on participation of at least 50% that is held for at least 365 calendar days and provided that the subsidiary company is not resident in a black-listed country (the list of which includes various non-treaty countries).

[408] Capital allowances for capital expenditures are available in the form of one-time deduction of up to 30% of the acquisition cost (up to 10% for fixed assets with a useful life of less than three years) and depreciation of the remainder over the useful life of the relevant fixed assets.

[409] The Russian taxation system includes large tax incentives (with regard to corporate profit tax and property tax and also, in certain business segments, with regard to mineral extraction tax and social security contributions) that are available (subject to specific conditions and procedures) for investments in special economic zones and various priority development areas, as well as for regional investment projects and investment projects covered by federal special investment contracts.

10.3 Tax Consolidation: Group Relief of Gains and Losses

[410] Profits and losses of a target can be consolidated within the purchaser's group only as part of the fiscal consolidation that, however, is available only to large corporate groups (that, on a consolidated basis, meet the following thresholds: aggregate amount of corporate profit tax, VAT, excise tax and mineral extraction tax of at least RUB10 bn, revenue of at least RUB100 bn and assets of at least RUB300 bn).

[411] Profits of a foreign subsidiary may be imputed to a Russian tax resident controlling parent company under Russian CFC rules (in effect since 2015, with the first taxation due as of 31 December 2016). For the purpose of the CFC rules, the controlling parent of a CFC is defined by reference to a specific participation threshold and the company's control over profit distribution. The relevant participation threshold is met if a person (together with his/her spouse and underage children) holds more than 10% and the participation of all Russian tax residents exceeds 50%; or if a person (together with his/her spouse and underage children) holds more than 25%. Unless distributed to the controlling parent company not later than by the end of the following calendar year, the profits of a CFC (if they exceed RUB100 m determined on a pro-rated basis) are included in the controlling parent's taxable income for such following calendar year. If distribution takes place after the CFC taxation occurred, then the controlling parent company will be exempted from tax on dividends.

[412] The exemption from profit taxation applies to a number of CFCs, namely: (A) entities that participate in mining projects on terms of production sharing, concession, license, service or another type of risk-sharing agreement signed with governments or organizations designated by the latter (whereby at least 90% of the participant's income derives from a project) (a 'mining project participant'); (B) entities that operate a new hydrocarbon offshore field (or hold a direct interest in such operator) ('operators of new offshore hydrocarbon fields'); (C) entities resident in a treaty country that issues bonds (either listed on a designated foreign stock exchange or recorded in a designated foreign clearing system) with a subsequent lending of proceeds to affiliates (whereby at least 90% of the issuer's expenses are made up of interest paid on bonds) ('bond issuers'); (D) active CFCs resident in a treaty country (except for those that do not participate in exchange of information), including: (i) companies if their passive income (e.g., dividends, interest, royalties, rentals, capital gains, fees from consulting and similar services) does not exceed 20% ('active companies'); (ii) holding companies in which a Russian controlling parent company holds at least a 75% interest for at least 365 calendar days and which, in turn, (a) holds for at least 365 days a participation interest of at least 50% in an active foreign company or at least a 75% participation interest in an active foreign sub-holding company, and (b) has passive income (other than dividends from active foreign companies and sub-holding companies) not exceeding 5% ('active holding companies'); (iii) sub-holding companies in which an active foreign holding company holds at least a 75% interest for at least 365 calendar days and which, in turn, (a) holds for at least 365 days at least a 50% participation interest in an active foreign company, and (b) has passive income (other than dividends from active foreign companies) not exceeding 5% ('active sub-holding companies').

[413] The CFC rules also apply to foreign structures such as trusts, foundations, funds, partnerships and other forms of collective investment or fiduciary management. By default, the settlor/founder is regarded as the controlling person of such 'structure' unless the structure is discretionary and non-revocable and the settlor/founder is not among the beneficiaries. Further, another person may be found to be the controlling person if he is empowered to control the distribution of income from the structure and, in addition, he has either the right to income from such structure or the right to dispose of its property or the right to receive its property upon liquidation of the structure.

10.4 Tax Considerations Regarding M&A Transactions

[414] The basic tax issues arising for the principal parties in an M&A transaction include, firstly, the taxability of income derived by the seller and, secondly, the assessment of the target company's tax liabilities and properly addressing those risks through pricing or the seller's warranties and indemnities.

[415] A corporate seller, that is, a Russian tax resident or a permanent establishment of a foreign company, is subject to 20% corporate profit tax on income derived from the disposal of shares/participatory interests less historical acquisition costs and other expenses incurred in connection with the sale. An individual seller that is resident in Russia is subject to 13% individual income tax on income from the disposal less acquisition costs and related expenses. For both corporate and individual sellers, the participation exemption of capital gains (introduced in 2011 for the first time) is applicable only with regard to a direct disposal of Russian shares/participatory interests and provided that the disposed shares/interests were acquired after 1 January 2011 and have been held for at least five years; furthermore, the shares may not be listed shares and no more than 50% of the underlying assets of the target can be real estate located in Russia. Exceptions apply to the disposal of shares in high-technology companies. Those shares may be listed shares and in addition (during the period until 2022), if they are listed (at least at the moment of disposal), then the minimum holding period is reduced to one year.

[416] A non-resident corporate seller of shares/participatory interests is subject to 20% corporate profit tax (on income from the disposal of shares/participatory interests less historical acquisition costs, determined in the currency of disposal) only if the shares/participatory interests (in Russian or non-Russian companies) derive (directly or indirectly) at least 50% of their value from immovable property located in Russia. The tax is payable by withholding by the purchaser and may be overridden by a tax treaty. A non-resident individual seller is subject to taxation in Russia only if the disposal is deemed to take place in Russia (which depends on a number of factors to be assessed in a particular case) that may be overridden by a tax treaty.

[417] The purchaser of shares/participatory interests is allowed to deduct its acquisition costs only at the moment of a future disposal. The target company's ability to continue loss carry-forward is not affected by a change of shareholders.

[418] In a disposal of assets, a corporate tax-resident seller is subject to 20% corporate profit tax on income derived from the disposal less post-depreciation book value of the assets. The purchaser may deduct the acquisition costs either by: (a) depreciation of each particular item of the acquired assets (in this case, the contract price is allocated among the assets acquired), or (b) if the disposal is structured as an enterprise deal, deduction of goodwill over five years and deduction of the remainder through depreciation of each particular item of the acquired assets (in this case, the purchaser is bound by the post-depreciation book value of the assets and treats the difference between the contract price and the aggregated book value as goodwill).

[419] When comparing enterprise deals with share deals, the former are more advantageous for the purchaser with regard to the deduction of the acquisition costs. One disadvantage, however, is the 20% VAT (which is a cash flow issue for the purchaser) and the capital gains tax burden which would normally arise for the seller.

[420] The price is negotiable. However, the corporate seller and purchaser may be obliged to make certain adjustments when determining the seller's income from the disposal or the purchaser's acquisition value. The adjustments are required, in particular, for listed shares if the contract price is outside of the minimum/maximum price range (as registered by a stock exchange or trading system); for non-listed shares if the contract price is outside of the +/-20% range of the imputed price (determined by acceptable valuation methods, including by the net asset per share method); and for participatory interest if the contract price is not compliant with the transfer pricing rules (that are broadly in line with the OECD Transfer Pricing Guidelines). Notably, with regard to shares and participatory interests, however, the transfer pricing rules apply only to transactions between affiliates (if certain value thresholds are exceeded). For transactions between individuals, it is also assumed that the pricing complies with the fair market value, although the Tax Code does not require adjustments for individual sellers. On the other hand, an individual purchaser is deemed to have derived taxable income (so-called material benefit) if (and to the extent) the contract price is below the fair market value (regardless of whether the transaction is with an affiliated party or not).

[421] Special price mechanisms (such as deferred payments, retentions, holdbacks and earn-outs) are common in Russian M&A transactions. However, none of these are dealt with in the Tax Code. In fact, the implementation of these mechanisms for corporate sellers is complicated since such sellers must determine their taxable income from the disposal as of the date when the title to shares/participatory interests is transferred; any subsequent price adjustment payments would require correction of the tax base and refilling of a corporate profit tax return (as well as penalties if applicable). On the other hand, individual sellers are subject to tax in the year when they receive payment for a disposal; hence, the implementation of these price mechanisms is less cumbersome.

[422] The disposal of shares/participatory interests for newly issued shares (often called 'disposal by way of in-kind contribution to the charter capital') enjoys the roll-over treatment (though with no step-up). The seller/transferor is not regarded as deriving income and is deemed to have acquired the newly issued shares at the acquisition value equalling the historical value of the disposed shares/interests. The purchaser is bound by the historical value of the acquired shares/interests (as such value was determined by the seller).

[423] Corporate reorganizations (in the form of transformation, accession, merger, spin-off and division) are tax neutral. However, debt pushdown through an accession (or merger) between the target company and the purchaser is unlikely to permit the continuation of interest deductions by the consolidated company.

10.5 Structuring the Investment

[424] Historically, investments in Russian businesses, Russian joint ventures and in most M&A transactions have been structured through foreign jurisdictions by taking advantage of English law (as the law governing the documentation) as well as by taking the benefits of Russian tax treaties. Projects by Russian investors have mostly been structured through a handful of the most commonly used treaty countries such as Cyprus (as well as Luxembourg and the Netherlands, though to a lesser extent). The tax advantages of such structures included the reduced tax treaty rate for dividends (5% instead of the standard 15% rate), exemption for interest and royalties, and the possibility to arrange for the full tax neutrality of the income from the disposal of shares/participatory interests. With the revisions of the Tax Code in 2015 (among others, the introduction of corporate tax residence rules, CFC rules (*see* paragraphs [392] and [403]) and the 'actual right to income' (beneficial ownership) concept (*see* paragraph [429]), all known as 'deoffshorization measures'), such historical structures have become more difficult to defend in tax audits.

[425] In order to neutralize the negative impact of the CFC rules and beneficial ownership concept for Russian tax residents that are the ultimate shareholders of such structures, the Tax Code provides for a look-through mechanism that permits the income paid by a Russian source to a foreign recipient to immediately be allocated to the taxable income of the ultimate Russian beneficiary.

10.6 Withholding Tax

[426] Payments to non-resident companies are subject to withholding tax. The withholding obligation is imposed on the payer of income that is either a Russian tax resident company or a Russian permanent establishment. The Tax Code does not regulate the issue of how the tax should be paid in the circumstances where the income is paid between two non-resident companies, neither of which is registered for tax purposes in Russia. In such instances, the parties to the transaction may decide to rely on the fact that the tax payment mechanism is not established by law; however, as a general principle, the tax obligation of the foreign income recipient would continue to exist.

[427] The Tax Code provides for a general 20% withholding tax assessed on the full amount of a person's income. The tax applies even if the income is paid in a material form or through an offset of counterclaims. There are special reduced rates for certain forms of income: 15% for dividend income and 15% for interest

paid on listed bonds issued by Russian legal entities in 2017–2021 and denominated in rubles. With regard to the disposal of immovable property located in Russia, the tax base can be reduced by the post-depreciation book value. With regard to services, the tax obligation (including through withholding) arises only if the service provider creates a permanent establishment in Russia.

[428] Russia has entered into multiple tax treaties (in 2019, eighty-three treaties in effect, covering eighty-four countries). Most of the treaties permit the reduction of Russian withholding taxes on dividends, interest and royalties; some treaties also create an exemption for income from the disposal of shares/participatory interests. The tax treaty relief can be obtained either in advance of the income payment or through a refund claim. Advance relief may be arranged by providing the payer of income with the recipient's tax residence certificate and, from 2017, with the recipient's confirmation that it has an 'actual right' (beneficial ownership) to specific income.

[429] As of 1 January 2015, the Tax Code defines the concept of 'actual right to income' (beneficial ownership of income). After a few revisions, this concept has been defined as follows: (a) A person is deemed to have an 'actual right to income' if he independently has the right, by virtue of direct or indirect shareholding, control or other circumstances, to use and/or dispose of income or if another person is authorized to do so; in this context, functions performed and risks undertaken by the person have to be taken into account; (b) a person is not deemed to have an 'actual right to income' if he has limited powers to dispose of income and performs intermediary functions for the benefit of another person (i.e., transfers the income received (or a part thereof) to a non-treaty eligible person, with no other functions performed and with no risks undertaken). Strictly speaking, only the definition in (b) is meant to apply in the circumstances where tax treaty relief is applicable. The definition in (a) is meant to apply only for the purposes of the Tax Code. The Russian tax authorities and courts are at the early stage of applying the 'actual right to income' (beneficial ownership) concept to tax treaty situations. So far, only a few cases resolved by the courts indicate that the tax authorities may exercise broader discretion in considering and evaluating the global corporate group structures and corporate governance and financing arrangements within such structures, proactively utilizing various instruments of international cooperation between tax authorities (including exchange of information).

10.7 Debt Financing

[430] The interest cost of an acquisition is generally deductible provided that the acquisition has a clear business reason and subject to the limits under transfer pricing rules and thin capitalization rules.

[431] The transfer pricing limits apply only if a loan qualifies as a controlled transaction under transfer pricing rules (i.e., where the lender and the borrower are related parties and certain value thresholds are exceeded). Furthermore, the Tax Code provides for the following safe-harbour interest rates: for ruble loans – the range of 0.75 to 1.25 multiplied by the Central Bank key rate (from 6 September 2019, the range is from 5.25% to 8.75%); for loans in JPY and CHF – the range of 2% to 5% plus the JPY/CHF LIBOR; for loans in other foreign currencies – the range of 4% to 7% plus the USD LIBOR (or where applicable, EURIBOR, SHIBOR, or GBP LIBOR).

10.8 Thin Capitalization

[432] The Russian thin capitalization rules were introduced in 2002, extended in 2005–2006, and significantly revised from 2017. The rules are triggered by a participation interest if it is held directly or indirectly by a controlling foreign shareholder (legal entity or individual) and exceeds 25% or 50% at each subsequent level in the chain of shareholdings (before 2017 the trigger was a more than 20% direct or indirect participation by a foreign legal entity). The rules mandate the specific debt/equity ratio of 3:1 generally and 12.5:1 for banks and financial lease companies. Any interest accrued on the controlled debt in excess of these ratios is deemed discriminatory. Borrowers cannot deduct excessive interest and, when paid, it is treated as the controlling foreign shareholder's dividend income (subject to 15% tax or a reduced treaty rate).

[433] These rules apply to 'controlled debt', which includes (in aggregate) any debt obtained from, or secured by, a controlling foreign shareholder or its Russian or foreign affiliates as well as debt that, though it does not meet the formal criteria, is aimed at arranging for ultimate payments to the controlling foreign shareholder or its affiliates (if so recognized by a court).

[434] The important 2017 revisions to the term 'controlled debt' are: (a) the extension of the term to debt obtained from, or secured by, foreign affiliates; (b) the introduction of the court's authority to recognize controlled debt; and (c) the introduction of a few important exceptions such as (i) debt owed to foreign bond issuers (under the same conditions as defined for the tax exemption under the CFC rules; *see* paragraph [403]); (ii) debt owed to Russian affiliates other than as a part of back-to-back arrangements with the controlling foreign shareholder or foreign affiliates; and (iii) debt owed to an unaffiliated bank (if no default and no enforcement against the controlling foreign shareholder or affiliates). Controlled debt that arose before 1 October 2014 benefits from special rules (in effect till 2019) that neutralize the negative effect of currency fluctuations.

10.9 Accounting Treatment

[435] Russian legal entities are obliged to maintain accounting books and prepare accounting statements in accordance with the principles laid down in the Law on

Accounting and in the Russian Accounting Standards (RAS) and relevant recommendations of the supervisory authority (the Ministry of Finance). In addition, certain types of companies (such as credit institutions, insurance companies, state-owned corporations, and listed joint stock companies) are obliged to prepare consolidated financial statements in accordance with the IFRS.

[436] Under the RAS, assets are accounted for at their historical acquisition value (exceptions: if acquired free-of-charge – at their fair market value; if acquired through in-kind contribution in exchange for newly issued shares – at the value determined by shareholders). For listed shares, the accounting should reflect the fair market value (by the end of each reporting period). Within a corporate reorganization (transformation, accession, merger, spin-off, division), the accounting can be made either at the historical value or the fair market value.

[437] Under the RAS, goodwill is recognized for accounting purposes only as a result of an enterprise deal (as the difference between the enterprise price and the aggregate of the asset value less liability value). Goodwill can be amortized over twenty years.

11 EMPLOYMENT CONSIDERATIONS

11.1 Legal Framework

[438] In Russia, certain fundamental labour rights are enshrined in the Russian Constitution, including the right to establish a trade union and the right to work in safe conditions, and regulated in detail by the Labor Code and other federal laws.

[439] The Labor Code, which came into effect in February 2002 (as further amended), replaced many unwieldy Soviet labour rules that had overwhelmingly favoured employees, and is more evenly balanced between the rights of employees and the reasonable needs of employers. The Labor Code defines the terms and conditions of employment in detail and its rules are compulsory for all employers (legal entities and individuals), Russian and foreign, who employ personnel in Russia.

[440] The Code of Administrative Violations complements and strengthens the Labor Code by establishing liability for violations of certain labour laws, such as those concerning collective bargaining, resolution of collective labour disputes and safety in the workplace. It gives courts the power to enforce the Labor Code, such as the authority to disqualify a chief executive who repeatedly violates labour law and prevent him from occupying a managerial position for up to three years.

[441] Numerous other federal laws deal with specific areas of labour law; regional and municipal legislation may also be applicable to employment relationships (particularly in health and safety).

[442] Employment relations are also regulated by internal regulations of the employer, collective bargaining agreements and individual employment contracts.

11.2 How Employment Aspects May Affect a Transaction

[443] The consent of employees or trade unions is not required for the sale of shares or change of control in a company, unless otherwise required by a collective bargaining agreement.

[444] However, the acquisition of a business may be followed by the restructuring of a company's operations, redundancy of personnel or transfer of certain employees to other positions within the company or within the purchaser's group. Sometimes, certain personnel arrangements may have to be implemented as pre-completion undertakings, such as reduction of headcount, ensuring continuation of employment of key employees.

[445] The CEO of a company can be replaced without prior notice by the relevant management body of the company (board of directors or shareholders meeting) subject to the payment of a severance of at least three average monthly salaries unless his or her employment contract provides for a higher amount. Termination of other employees is subject to the redundancy rules discussed below.

[446] In Russia, redundancy is heavily regulated, and failure to observe the applicable procedure may lead to reinstatement of the dismissed employee, payment of compensation for the period starting from his/her termination until his/her reinstatement, and compensation of moral damages.[124] Furthermore, the employees to be made redundant must not belong to any category of employees who enjoy special protection against redundancy pursuant to Russian law (e.g., mothers of children under 3 years of age). Priority rights of certain categories of employees for continuation of employment must also be observed when only some of the employees who occupy the same position are being made redundant.

[447] Employees can be terminated in such cases only if it is impossible to transfer them to another position within the company, which an employee agrees to and is suitable for (including positions for which the employee may be overqualified).[125] Further, the employee must receive two months' notice prior to the termination of employment. Earlier termination can only occur with the consent of the employee. Russian law also requires notifying the Russian employment authorities on upcoming redundancy at least two months in advance or three months in advance for group redundancy as defined by Russian law. The company is also required to give two months' written notice to any trade unions in the company, or at least three months' notice if the termination of employment may lead to group redundancy.

[124] Articles 3 and 394 of the Labor Code; para. 63 of the Resolution of the Supreme Court No. 2 'On Application of the Labor Code by the Courts of the Russian Federation' dated 17 March 2004.

[125] Article 180 of the Labor Code. Paragraph 29 of the Supreme Court's Resolution on the Labor Code.

Employment of employees who are members of a trade union may be terminated on the basis of redundancy only upon consultations with the trade union pursuant to the procedure established by the Russian Labor Code. Termination of employment on the basis of redundancy requires the payment of a severance in the amount of up to three average monthly salaries unless a larger severance payment is established by the collective bargaining agreement, internal regulations of the company or individual employment agreements.

[448] It is also common to retain and ensure the cooperation of certain key employees whose contribution is required for the transaction to be effectively implemented and closed. Sometimes, the employment of certain key employees is necessary for some time post-completion in order to ensure the smooth transfer of the business to a new owner. Such employees usually include top managers, chief financial officers and legal personnel; other key employees may be industry specific. In order to ensure their effective work pre-completion (or as the case may be – post-completion), the company may offer to pay bonuses dependent on (i) continuation of their employment, (ii) the achievement of certain key performance indicators (KPIs), and (iii) closing of the transaction.

[449] In addition, change of control may result in additional payments to the employees if such payments are required by incentive plans, collective bargaining agreement, internal regulations of the company or by the individual employment agreements.

[450] It would be not unusual for a company to enter into non-competition and/or non-solicitation agreements with the key employees whose employment is being terminated; however, a non-competition and/or non-solicitation undertaking would be difficult to enforce in Russia.

[451] Under the Russian Labor Code, one of the main principles in the regulation of labour relations is the freedom of labour, which includes the right to work, the right to make free use of one's abilities for work and to choose an occupation and type of activity.[126] Although employment agreements may regulate an existing employment relationship, they may not contain any conditions which could interfere with the employee's rights and guarantees established by Russian labour law.[127] Since non-competition clauses hinder an employee's rights as established by Russian labour law, they are not enforceable in Russia.

[452] Russian employment law is silent with respect to non-solicitation arrangements as such, allowing Russian courts to turn to Russian civil law using the principle of analogy. Although the Russian Civil Code[128] recognizes that a promise to refrain from taking certain actions may constitute a civil law obligation, the Civil Code does not permit the limitation of the legal capacity of an individual or a legal

[126] Article 2 of the Labor Code; Art. 37 of the Constitution of the Russian Federation, adopted 12 December 1993.

[127] Article 9 of the Labor Code.

[128] Article 307 of the Civil Code.

entity by contract unless provided by law.[129] Furthermore, the Civil Code provides that the waiver of civil law rights by individuals and legal entities does not terminate those rights,[130] unless otherwise specified by law. Thus, it may be argued that a contractual obligation to refrain from taking certain actions in cases that are not expressly addressed by Russian law is not enforceable. Further, given that the Civil Code (i) explicitly allows individuals and legal entities to enter into contracts freely,[131] and (ii) precludes the abuse of a legal right and stipulates that the exercise of civil law rights for the purpose of limiting competition (which may be viewed as one of the reasons for entering into a non-solicitation arrangement) is not permitted.[132] Therefore, even if a party agrees to a non-solicitation clause in a contract, it will likely be unenforceable insofar as it limits competition and impairs the right to freely enter into contracts with other parties.[133] Under Russian employment law, employers may not refuse to enter into an employment contract with a candidate whose skills and qualifications meet the requirements established by the employer or by law for a specific position.[134] Since a non-solicitation undertaking also implies an obligation, among others, not to hire certain candidates for reasons not relevant to their professional qualifications, such undertaking may be viewed as contradicting Russian labour law, or even discriminatory, and therefore may be deemed unenforceable.

11.3 General Employment Principles in Russia

[453] Russian law prohibits the conclusion of civil law agreements that in fact regulate employment relations between an employee and the employer. The employer and employee must execute a written employment contract setting out the basic terms and conditions of employment. The employer must prepare the written contract and offer it to the prospective employee, and two original contracts (one for the employer and one for the employee) should be signed by both within three days from the first date of employment (e.g., from the date when the employee actually started to work). Once the employment contract has been signed by both parties, the employer must issue a formal order hiring the employee within three days and present it to the employee for signature.

[454] As a general rule, neither the employer nor the employee can amend the essential terms and conditions of an employment agreement without the other's consent. Furthermore, the provisions of an employment contract are invalid if they attempt to exclude or restrict the employee's rights guaranteed by the Labor Code. In the event of a dispute, the employer bears the burden of proof of establishing the essential terms and conditions of the employment contract.

[129] Articles 22(3) and 49(2) of the Civil Code.
[130] Article 9(2) of the Civil Code.
[131] Article 421 of the Civil Code.
[132] Article 10(1) of the Civil Code.
[133] Article 421 of the Civil Code.
[134] Article 64 of the Labor Code.

[455] Unilateral termination of an employment contract by the employer is possible only in cases which are expressly provided for by the Labor Code and mainly include the termination of employment for different causes. Russian law generally allows work force reduction following a strict procedure and subject to the provision of guarantees to all employees who are made redundant and special protection which the Labor Code grants to certain categories of employees. Statutory employee rights, benefits or protections may not be waived or contracted out or derogated.

[456] The employment of some categories of senior managers is subject to special regulation under Russian law. Thus, employees who serve as sole executive bodies (e.g., CEO, general director, president) as well as members of collective executive bodies (e.g., members of a management board) are appointed on the basis of a resolution of the authorized governing body of a company.

[457] Employment agreements with the head of a company are concluded for a term specified in the employer's foundation documents (e.g., articles of association). The head of a company may also work for another organization only subject to the consent of the relevant governing body of the employer. The head of a company is fully liable for any direct, actual damage he or she causes. As a general rule, he is also liable for losses caused by his culpable actions or omissions.

[458] The members of the board (i.e., members of collective executive bodies) may enjoy the same employment-related rights as the head of the company only if the company's foundation documents so allow.

[459] Non-competition or non-solicitation clauses, which are often included in employment agreements with senior management in other jurisdictions, are not enforceable in Russia, although in practice they are common.

[460] As a general rule, non-Russian citizens may not work in Russia without a work permit. Obtaining a work permit is usually a time-consuming and complex process. Different procedures are applied with respect to foreign citizens who come to Russia on a visa basis and those who enter Russia without an obligation to obtain a visa. Work permits are valid for a term of up to one year and only within the territory of the constituent entity of the Russian Federation for which they are issued. Before their expiration, work permits may be reissued for a new term not exceeding one year (for foreign citizens who do not require a visa to come to Russia, a work permit may be reissued for a new term only once).

[461] As of 1 July 2010, a new simplified and expedited procedure for obtaining a work permit for so-called highly qualified specialists was introduced. Under Russian law, highly qualified specialists are people whose monthly salary under their Russian employment with a particular Russian employer and that apply for a work permit equals or exceeds RUB167 000 (approximately EUR2 400) and who has certain experience, skills or achievements in specific areas. For certain categories of foreign citizens, the monetary threshold may be lower. A work permit for a highly qualified specialist may be issued for a term of up to three years (and may be extended for a new term not exceeding three years).[135]

[462] As of 10 January 2014, some categories of foreign citizens may apply for a work permit on the basis of a simplified and expedited procedure. These include foreign citizens who are seconded for work in the Russian Federation by a foreign commercial organization registered in a country which is a member of the WTO in order to work in:

- a Russian subsidiary of the foreign commercial organization, if the main activity of the Russian subsidiary is the provision of services; or
- branch or a representative office of such foreign commercial organization.

[463] This simplified procedure may apply only if the foreign citizens have been employed by the foreign commercial organization for at least one year prior to their secondment, and are seconded to: (a) a representative office to perform management and coordination of the representative office's activity, or (b) a branch or Russian subsidiary as key personnel (i.e., the head of the branch or Russian subsidiary, or other positions the salary for which is at least RUB2 m (approximately, EUR28 600) per year and provided that foreign employees have high qualifications and/or extraordinary knowledge meeting the requirements established by the Government of the Russian Federation, and such qualification and knowledge are needed for the provision of services by the branch or the Russian subsidiary.

[464] Citizens of the Republic of Belarus, Republic of Kazakhstan or Republic of Armenia may work in Russia without a work permit.

11.4 Trade Unions

[465] Under Russian law, employees are entitled to representation for the protection of their rights and interests in connection with their individual and collective labour relations. As a general rule, employees are represented by trade unions. Although trade unions are generally not common in small or middle size businesses (and it is not common for an employer to negotiate a collective bargaining agreement with employees of such businesses), in large companies or in certain industries (such as the automotive industry) trade unions are common and very influential.

[466] A union may be formed by employees who: (i) are over 14 years old, and (ii) work (as a rule) for the same company. If the employees do not work in the same company, they may still be members of the same union. A union may be formed by at least three employees. To establish a union, such employees, i.e., its founders, must hold a general foundation meeting. State registration of a union as a legal entity is optional.

[135] Federal Law No. 115-FZ 'On Legal Status of Foreign Citizens in the Russian Federation' dated 25 July 2002.

[467] Any employee (including a foreign citizen residing in Russia, unless otherwise specified by a federal law or international treaty of the Russian Federation) may freely join a trade union without prior consent from the employer and/or a state authority.

[468] As a general rule, a union represents a group of employees who are members of the trade union (save for certain cases of collective bargaining negotiations and agreements, and resolution of collective labour disputes). However, employees who are not members of a trade union may authorize a trade union's bodies to represent their interests in their relations with the employer. Russian law does not establish any specific membership threshold requirement for a union to be recognized by the employer.

[469] The employer must consult with the union in cases provided by law, internal regulations or collective bargaining agreements. For example, the employer must consult with the union when requesting employees to work overtime, during weekends or holidays, when approving a vacation schedule, terminating the employment of union members, etc. An employer may still proceed with the above actions despite union opposition; however, in such a case, those actions may be challenged by the relevant employment authorities or in court.

[470] When laying off employees, the employer must notify the union about the commencement of the layoff process at least two months in advance (at least three months in advance for group layoffs); however, if the laid-off employees are not members of a union, the employer is not required to request the union's opinion.

[471] If more than half of the employees of a company belong to a union, it may petition for the conclusion of a collective bargaining agreement which will apply to all the employees of the company. If the number of union members is less than one-half of the company's employees, a general meeting (conference) of employees may be convened and the union or any other employee representatives may be elected to start the collective bargaining procedure with the company.

11.5 Employee Option Plans

[472] The most commonly used benefits to attract or retain key employees or top managers are employee option plans.

[473] Russian labour laws should not generally impact option plans so long as participation in the plan is not considered to be a benefit provided by a Russian employer pursuant to an employment relationship (e.g., when the option plan is offered not by the Russian employer, but by the foreign parent company of the employer, and is governed by foreign law). On the other hand, participation in the plan can be connected to (and is conditional upon) the employees' relations with the Russian employer. Therefore, the enforceability of option plans may be subject to their compliance with Russian labour laws and their inclusion in Russian employment documentation.

[474] Russian law generally prohibits the acquisition of foreign securities or foreign financial instruments which have not been admitted to public trade in Russia by persons who are not qualified investors (e.g., employees). However, pursuant to the regulations of Federal Service for Financial Markets this restriction does not apply if such securities or financial instruments are acquired by Russian citizens under their employment contract or in connection with the fulfilment of duties under the employment contract. Although Russian law generally allows employees to acquire securities, it is still unclear whether an employee can be offered foreign securities or financial instruments in Russia.

[475] When structuring and implementing employee option plans, a number of issues need to be considered, including, among others, currency control and compliance with the requirements for personal data protection.

www.ingramcontent.com/pod-product-compliance
Lightning Source LLC
Chambersburg PA
CBHW071354230926
51846CB00002B/546
9789403527635